Witchcraft
on a
Shoestring

Practicing the Craft Without
Breaking Your Budget

Witchcraft
on a
Shoestring

Practicing the Craft Without Breaking Your Budget

Deborah Blake

Chicago, Illinois

First Printing. 2023.

Paperback ISBN: 978-1-959883-19-7
Library of Congress Control Number on file.

Cover design by Wycke Malliway.
Interior illustrations by Wycke Malliway.
Typesetting by Gianna Rini.
Edited by Becca Fleming.

Published by:
Crossed Crow Books, LLC
6934 N Glenwood Ave, Suite C
Chicago, IL 60626
www.crossedcrowbooks.com

Printed in the United States of America.

DEDICATION

As always, this book is dedicated to the wonderful women of Blue Moon Circle, and our extended circle of family, friends, and fellow travelers. I couldn't do it without you, and I wouldn't want to. And special thanks to Robin and Shannon for all their writing help!

To all the writers who share this journey with me—you inspire and support me, and I continue to learn from you every day. Special thanks to Raven Digitalis, Ellen Dugan, Gail Wood, Edain McCoy, Christopher Penczak, Denise Dumars, and the fabulous Z. Budapest. You set the bar high!

With special thanks to Bryanna and my father, both of whom suggested the idea of doing this book to me at about the same time…making me think it *must* be a good topic!

And to my readers, who also inspire and encourage me. Thanks for your continued emails, letters, and feedback. This one's for you!

CONTENTS

Chapter 5
The Crafty Witch:
Thirty-Five Simple and Thrifty Craft Projects for Magickal Purposes *66*

WOOD

PAPER

GLASS

STONE

CHAPTER 6
FEEDING THE MASSES:
FORTY-FIVE FEAST DISHES FOR LESS   136

IMBOLC

OSTARA

BELTANE

LITHA

LAMMAS

MABON

SAMHAIN

FULL MOON CAKES & ALE

CAKES

ALE

CHAPTER 7
FIFTY WAYS TO PRACTICE WITCHCRAFT FOR LITTLE OR NO MONEY 184

CHAPTER 8
THE EVERYDAY WITCH– WHEN BEING A WITCH DOESN'T MEAN BUYING MORE STUFF 193

INTRODUCTION

Practicing Witchcraft can be expensive. I've heard this complaint from fellow Pagans for years. A good cloak can cost well over a hundred dollars, for instance. Then there is the cost of the Supplies: herbs, gemstones, candles, statuary, pentacles, and tools like athames and wands. It is easy to spend hundreds of dollars on the Craft without even trying. And that's before you start buying the books (my own particular weak point, as you might imagine).

Most Pagans are not wealthy folks, and these days, many of us have less "extra" money than we've had in years. Times are tough. But we still want to practice our Craft to the best of our ability. What's a Witch to do?

Well, you can do what my friends in Blue Moon Circle and I have been doing since we started our coven in the spring of 2004—working Witchcraft on a shoestring.

Witchcraft on a shoestring is as much an attitude as it is a way to save money. We approach our practice of the Craft much as we deal with the rest of our lives: making the most out of what we have, creating something out of not very much, and spending as little money as possible to achieve the end result we want. In short—we're cheap.

But not necessarily easy.

Sometimes, practicing Witchcraft on a shoestring requires extra effort. For instance, instead of buying that fancy cloak, you can sew one yourself. And you have to learn to think outside the box. Just because the wands in your favorite catalog are made of silver and topped with gemstones doesn't mean that a lovely piece of wood you found in the forest won't work just as well.

I'll talk about all these things within the pages of this book. We'll start with a discussion on the bare-bones basics of a Witchcraft practice, work our way through which items are really necessary (and which are extras to indulge in when you can), and talk about inexpensive substitutes for more commonly used expensive items (like the cloaks and wands I mentioned earlier).

You'll also find chapters on simple craft projects and recipes for inexpensive feast food. And finally, I'll list fifty suggestions for ways to practice your Craft for free or practically free. I don't know about you, but the Blue Mooners and I are big fans of free!

Some of these options may be new to you. Others may be things you've been doing for years (in which case, give yourself a pat on the back—you're already well on your way). Not every suggestion will be right for every Witch, of course, so pick and choose the ones that work the best for you and your practice.

Most of all, remember to have fun. After all, Witchcraft at its core is a combination of "reverence and mirth." And as any child knows, it doesn't cost anything to laugh.

We can worship our gods and follow the Pagan path without emptying our wallets or maxing out our credit cards. It just takes a little extra work, some imagination, a touch of magick, and voila! You're practicing Witchcraft on a shoestring.

CHAPTER 1

THE ONLY TOOLS YOU NEED ARE FREE: BELIEF, WILL, AND FOCUS

People often ask me, "What tools do you need to practice Witchcraft?" I know that they're thinking of things like athames, wands, pentacles, and the like, and they expect me to give them a long shopping list of "must-have" equipment.

And there are certainly lots of tools you *can* use in your practice of the Craft. There are tools that make it easier to cast a spell, help to focus and direct energy, aid in divination, and assist in various aspects of organizing and accumulating knowledge.

But there are only *two* things you truly need to practice Witchcraft—and they're both free.

No, I'm not kidding.

To follow the Pagan path, all you *really* need is your heart and your mind.

Witchcraft, from my own perspective and practice, is a nature-based religion, most often involving both a Goddess and a God (although sometimes only a Goddess, and often multiple deities). To some, Witchcraft isn't considered a religion at all and is instead a practice of magickal craft excluding the influence of any deity. It follows the seasonal and lunar cycles, is based at least in part on ancient Pagan practices, and is strongly rooted in the concepts of personal responsibility and the power of magick to create positive change.

None of those things require a black velvet cloak or a silver wand.

To be a Witch, all you really require is faith. Faith in yourself and in whichever gods you follow. And if you practice with others, it helps to have faith in them, too. (We call that "perfect love and perfect trust.")

So where do the cloak and the wand—and all the other tools of Witchcraft—come in?

As I mentioned, many Witches actively pursue the work of magick. And magick, while it can be performed without anything other than your heart and mind, is often easier and more powerful if you have a few tools to aid your efforts.

Different Witches favor the use of different tools. For instance, I use an athame, but not a wand. Not that there is anything wrong with using a wand—it is a handy tool for directing energy—but I tend to use my athame for that and have never felt the need for an additional tool.

But all Witches who practice magick in one form or another will eventually utilize three basic tools: belief, will, and focus. And yes, they're all free, too.

BELIEF

At the root of all magick, we have the belief that magick truly works. Not in a "Harry Potter, wave a wand and presto" kind of way, but in a "this is a law of nature" way.

Unlike most folks, Witches believe in magick: the power to change the world around us through the focused application of will and energy. Without this belief, our words would have no power and that wand would simply be a piece of wood.

With belief, however, comes the ability to tap into the energy of the universe and manipulate "reality"—not necessarily in drastic and dramatic ways (although that can happen too), but mostly by giving the world a nudge in the right direction.

With our strong belief behind it, that piece of wood becomes a tool to guide the energy of our intent, summon the elements, or sketch out a sacred symbol. The wand is what you might call a "power enhancer." The real tool in use here is our belief that magick is real and that we can make it work for us.

WILL

If belief is the primary tool of Witchcraft, then will is the engine that powers it. Without our will, our belief just kinda sits there. It looks pretty and sounds good, but it doesn't actually achieve anything. You can talk about your beliefs until the cows come home, but if you never fuel them with your will, then, magickally at least, it is all still just talk.

To work magick, we take our belief in the possibility of creating positive change through magickal means and apply the directed power of our will and intent to make it happen. This usually means setting a goal (increasing prosperity, for example), creating a spell or ritual of some kind that will help us achieve that goal, and concentrating all our will on our intention to bring that goal to fruition.

FOCUS

Focus is the act of directing that will to give our magick power. The more focus you have, the more of your will is directed into the magick you work, and the more powerful it will be. Most of the tools we use as Witches are intended to boost or reinforce our focus as we work a spell, therefore giving us more power and a greater likelihood of succeeding at our task.

For instance, when doing prosperity magick, we may use a green candle, inscribe it with symbols to signify money and abundance, anoint it with "money drawing" oil, and say the spell on a Thursday. All these elements are thought by some to be connected with prosperity, so they may help to hone our focus on the work at hand.

So, what does any of this have to do with practicing Witchcraft on a shoestring, and what do I mean when I say, "the only tools you need are free"?

Well, obviously, in the example I mentioned above, there are a couple of tools that cost something: the candle, for instance, and the special oil. When we get to the section on crafting your own tools, I'll show you a few ways to use these things without spending as much—but the truth is, you don't *need* to spend anything at all.

At the heart of any spell or ritual for prosperity are the three tools that every Witch already possesses: belief, will, and focus. With these, you can create magick for anything you desire. If you believe you can bring more prosperity into your life, if you will it to be so, and focus that will with all your might—you have all that you require to create magick. Write your spell on a piece of paper or speak to the gods from your heart, and you have sent magick out into the universe.

I'm not saying that you should never use a candle or add a boost to your magickal work in other ways. I have all sorts of tools that I use to help focus my power; I've even spent money on some of them.

What I *am* saying is that while such things can be useful, helpful, and even fun to add to a magickal practice, you can be a Witch without them. It is up to you—and your budget—how many "extras" you throw into your magickal pot.

In the end, the only tools you really need are belief, will, and focus. And they are yours to use for free, with the power of your heart and mind, and the blessings of the gods.

CHAPTER 2

KNOWLEDGE IS POWER:
BOOKS, RESEARCH, AND SHARING
KNOWLEDGE

Sir Francis Bacon said, "Knowledge is power" (Sacred Meditations, Of Heresies. 1597). And he was right. This statement is true for life in general, but it is especially true in Witchcraft.

I mean this in a universal sense; in that the more you know about Witchcraft, the better you are able to "walk your talk" and integrate your Pagan beliefs into your mundane life. Knowledge is almost always a good thing. But I also mean it in a specific way as well: the more you know, the less likely you are to make mistakes or just plain get it wrong.

What can I say? I'm speaking from experience here.

One fact of magickal living that many long-time Witches will tell you is that when they were first following the path, they occasionally had a spell not go the way they intended . Most often, this just means the spell didn't work. Sometimes, however, the end result can be unpleasant—the magick works, but in a way that is destructive or unintentionally harmful to you or others. Love spells are the easiest to get wrong, especially when you are just starting out. And when they backfire, you can get stuck with someone you don't want, with no good way to get rid of them. But any spell can either fizzle out or go awry if you aren't careful with your words and clear in your intent.

The best way to avoid this is to make sure you have all the information you need before working magick. This means gathering as much knowledge as you can.

Additionally, many Witches (including me) believe that one of the main goals of being a Witch is to become the best person you can be. Learning and growing are a big part of the journey to self-improvement, which is where the less specific (non-magickal) knowledge comes in.

So, how do we gather all this knowledge—thus increasing our own power—without dramatically decreasing our bank accounts?

There are three primary routes that most Witches travel to accumulate knowledge: books, the Internet, and other Witches.

BOOKS

I'm going to start off this section by suggesting that you do something contrary to the theme of this book— spend money.

Okay, okay, don't throw things at me. Allow me to explain.

For one thing, obviously, I am an author. I want you to buy my books! But additionally, if people don't spend money on books at least part of the time, Pagan authors won't write them, and we'll be missing out on a lot of knowledge we might have no other way to access. It is also nice to build up a stock of books that contain the information you need to refer to the most often. If you write your own spells and rituals, for instance, you will want to have at least a couple of books on correspondences.

This doesn't mean you need to run out and buy every book on Wicca, Witchcraft, or Paganism you see, however. Take the time to consider which books you want to have a place in your own personal Pagan library.

Most Witches have different areas of study that appeal to them and different needs when it comes to magickal practice. But most of us want to have at least one or two books on the following subjects: Witchcraft basics, herbs, gemstones, rituals and spellcasting, Sabbats and lunar lore, history, classics and traditional practices, gods and goddesses, personal practice, correspondences and reference, and advanced learning. (See the end of this section for some of my favorites in each of these categories to get you started on building your library if you don't have one already.)

Of course, that can add up to a lot of books (at least it does in my house), so you will probably want to find alternatives to buying them all new. Here are a few "Witchcraft on a shoestring" tips for finding books on the cheap.

THE LIBRARY—For books you only need on a temporary basis, the library is a great place to start. It is free, most of us have one located fairly near us, and you can use an interlibrary loan to request books that your own library doesn't have in their collection. The biggest drawback to the library, where most of us are concerned, is that they often don't have a large collection of Pagan or Witchcraft books available. In part, that is because there is less demand for such books (or they think there is) or because of censorship. But it is also an unfortunate truth that Witchcraft books are among the most often stolen out of libraries, so they simply stop buying them. Let me say for the record that theft is *not* a good way to get free books. Seriously bad karma, people. You can, however, request that your library purchase a particular book. (Mine, for instance. Hint, hint.) If there is enough interest in a title or an author, they might just do it.

Your friends—If you have friends who are also Pagans, you can always swap books with each other. That way, each of you can buy fewer books and spread them around. I do suggest, however, that you only do this with people you are certain will return the books they borrow from you or with titles you don't particularly care if you get back or not. Be sure to write your name on the inside of any book you want returned to you, and you might want to write down who you loaned it to, for good measure. You can also pass on books you're done with; sometimes we outgrow certain books (like beginner introductions to magick) or just didn't find them appealing. Someone else might still be able to get some use out of them.

Online book swaps—There are a number of places online that are dedicated to swapping books that people are finished reading (this is a permanent swap—you don't get your books back). Most of these involve signing up, listing the books you have available, and which books you are looking for. Usually, the only cost involved is in mailing the books, and if you use "book rate" at the post office, that can be much cheaper. You can try *paperbackswap.com* and *BookMooch.com*. And there are sites that do swapping in general, where you can look for books, like *Freecycle.org*.

Another online source for inexpensive books is the ever-popular eBay. There are plenty of Pagan books available there at prices that start at pennies per title. You can also sometimes buy a group of books for not much money in which case you can pick out the ones you want to keep and share the rest.

While you're looking for book bargains, don't forget to check your local used bookstore. There may not be as many Witchcraft titles available there, but at least you won't have to pay to have them mailed, and you can sometimes turn in books you are finished with and get some money off of whichever ones you are buying.

Big retailers, like Barnes and Noble, often run sales and specials. You can sign up online or at the stores themselves and get an email notification whenever there is a sale. They often email you coupons as well. What's not to like?

Don't forget your local independent bookstore, Pagan store, or New Age Store. These folks sometimes run specials, too (or will give you a deal if you buy a bunch), and then you are supporting your local small businessperson—always a good thing. If you keep your eyes open, you might even find an author's book signing, so you can meet one of your favorite writers in person. The book may not be on sale, but it is fun to collect the signatures of authors you like and respect.

Bookstores and Pagan suppliers often sell older and/or discontinued titles at a discount. Check out catalogs or look online. A couple of the ones I use the most are Azure Green and Isis Books, both of which have online listings. Some publishers also run specials online on older titles or Annuals for the past year.

Yard sales are another good place to look for used books. It may be harder to find titles on Witchcraft, but one of the women in Blue Moon Circle has a remarkable collection she has accumulated over the years from the many yard sales she's been to. Sometimes it pays to wander around aimlessly on a Saturday morning!

One place you might not think to look is on an author's website. Some authors occasionally run contests on their blogs or websites and give away free books. If there is someone in particular you like, you might want to check periodically to see if they are promoting a new book by having a contest or giveaway. If you follow authors on social media, they usually post about such events in those places.

As you can see, there are probably more resources than you ever dreamed of for finding free, cheap, or less-expensive books on Witchcraft, Paganism, or any other knowledge you need. So, there is no excuse for not having a library of treasured books to return to again and again.

On the other hand, when you only need a little information or you need to know something right away and don't happen to have a book on that topic, you can turn to another source—the Internet.

The Internet

The Internet is a great source of information. All you have to do is type in what you are looking for, and presto, knowledge for the taking. Say, for instance, you are writing a Summer Solstice ritual for your Pagan friends. You will be able to find how the holiday was celebrated in earlier times, which gods and goddesses are traditionally associated with the Solstice, what kinds of magick are typically practiced on that day, and even entire rituals and recipes. And it's all free. Who could ask for more?

There is one problem with the information available on the Internet, however (besides the fact that you can easily spend all day looking up fun facts and not get anything else done). A lot of it is crap.

Seriously.

For every piece of good information you find, there is another bit that is misleading, confusing, or just plain wrong. Many so-called experts post entire sites full of stuff they've made up, more or less from nothing, and call it fact. And it can be hard to tell the real knowledge from the delusional ramblings, sometimes. Much-used sites like Wikipedia, for instance, contain information from many different people; anyone can go onto a posted article and add or change the information. So, what looks like truth may end up being completely correct, partially correct, or a load of cow plop.

This doesn't mean that the Internet can't be a good place to look for knowledge. I use it all the time. I even used it to look up some of the information included in this book, like the online sites for book swapping. What it does mean, however, is that you may have to spend more time and energy double and even triple-checking your facts before you can be certain that the information you've found is accurate. As I said before, sometimes free requires a little extra work.

Over time, you will undoubtedly find some consistently reliable sites; ones you can return to time after time. This can make the task of chasing down knowledge easier. Make sure the source is legitimate, that the person who has posted the information is credible, and that their information matches up with most of whatever else you are finding on the topic. And remember to use common sense and listen to your own inner wisdom. If something you read online doesn't sound right to you, it probably isn't.

To get you started, here are a few places to look online:

AUTHOR WEBSITES. If there is an author whose writing you respect and enjoy, you can check their websites to see if they have any additional information posted. Many Pagan authors have excerpts from their books, spells or rituals, general information on Witchcraft, and links to other useful sites.

Publishers. For instance, Crossed Crow Books has a website and social media accounts with information on topics such as astrology, tarot, and magick.

Online Pagan magazines. One of my favorites is "The Wiccan/Pagan Times," which can be found at *wicpagtimes.com*. Another, which is a combination of blog and magazine, is *The Magical Buffet* at *themagicalbuffet.com*. BBI Media, which puts out the fabulous print magazines *Sage Woman* and *Witches & Pagans* (was *newWitch* and *PanGaia*) has excerpts from some of their issues online—although I warn you, you'll probably get hooked and want to subscribe.

Websites and/or blogs that are primarily intended to provide information. Some of these also sell books or supplies, provide links, or specialize in Pagan book reviews.

Websites that provide (for a fee, sometimes) classes on Wicca and Witchcraft. These may teach a particular path or approach, and the cost can vary from free to quite expensive. Remember to check to make sure that a site is legitimate, especially if it is asking for money. Here are a couple of popular sites:

- *paganpath.com* (Pagan Path)
- *witchschool.com* (Witch School International)

This is just the tip of the iceberg, of course. I could write an entire book just on Internet sources of information. The problem with that (other than the fact that it would be a really boring book) is the transient nature of many websites and blogs.

The ones I've listed here have been around for a while at the time that I write this and will hopefully still be around by the time you read it. But sites on the Internet come and go at the speed of light as the people who put them up lose interest, get side-tracked by life, or simply run out of things to say. So, it is a good idea to have other places to go for information in case your favorite site has disappeared right when you need the answer to a pressing question. A great alternative to books and websites may be right around the corner, on the other end of the phone line, or at a Pagan networking site.

OTHER WITCHES

About half of what I know about Witchcraft, I learned from books. The other half I got more directly from other Witches. I have been fortunate enough to live in a community that, despite its relatively small size, has a number of Pagans. And these folks have been, for the most part, both willing and able to share with me their extensive body of knowledge. Without them, I wouldn't be the Witch I am today.

My recommendation is that you seek out other Witches if you can. They don't have to be famous authors or high priests and high priestesses—we all have insights, knowledge, and thoughts that are worth sharing with each other.

Nor do these other folks have to share your exact path in order to have wisdom worth sharing. I have learned some amazing things from Pagans and Witches who practice very different styles of Witchcraft from mine.

It can be hard to find other people who follow the Craft. You can try asking anyone you know who is Pagan-sympathetic if they know of people who practice. You can check the notice boards at local health food or New Age stores in case someone has posted an invitation to an open ritual. There might even be one in the newspapersince some Witches meet out of Unitarian Universalist churches.

Of course, if you are lucky enough to live in a town that has a Pagan store, you can just go in and talk to whoever is behind the counter. But if none of these approaches work for you—or if you are not ready to come out of the broom closet and need a method that allows for more anonymity, you can take your search for other Witches online.

There are a number of social media sites especially for Witches and Pagans. If you go to social media sites, such as Facebook or Twitter, you should have no problem finding someone to talk to there!

In addition, many Pagan authors and leaders can be found on social media (including me). Most of these folks are happy to talk to fans and Witches with inquiring minds and will answer questions as their time and workloads allow.

This brings us to the question of etiquette when dealing with other Witches, especially those you don't know well, or any you contact online (*never* call someone you don't know, unless you have been given their number by a mutual acquaintance or they themselves have given you permission). Here are a few things to keep in mind in your pursuit of knowledge from other Witches:

NEVER ASSUME THAT A WITCH IS OUT OF THE BROOM CLOSET OR COMFORTABLE TALKING ABOUT PAGAN TOPICS IN FRONT OF OTHER PEOPLE. Unless you are in a situation where it is obvious that an open conversation is acceptable (such as at a ritual, in a Pagan store, or when talking to someone who is well known for their Pagan activities), try and be discreet about asking questions. If possible, wait until you are in a reasonably private conversation before bringing up the subject, unless you know for a fact that the person you are talking to is open about their practice of the Craft.

BE RESPECTFUL OF OTHER PEOPLE'S PRIVACY AND SECRETS. Some people are very happy to share their personal practices, but others still follow the old ways and don't discuss their magickal work with anyone. If another Witch doesn't wish to talk about their practice, that is their right and should be accepted without argument.

IF YOU WRITE TO AN AUTHOR OR PAGAN LEADER, BE CONSIDERATE. Be sure to type clearly, since they probably have to read a lot of messages and emails. Most authors can be contacted through their publishers. Be aware that these folks are likely to be extremely busy and may or may not be able to answer every email or go into detail in answer to a question.

IF YOU DISAGREE WITH WHAT ANOTHER PAGAN WRITES ON A BLOG OR WEBSITE, DO SO POLITELY. It is never okay to write an email or response to a blog post that attacks or denigrates another Witch. If you must disagree (and there are some discussions where disagreement is inevitable), do so *nicely*, with respect for all those involved. You are entitled to your opinion and so is everyone else.

IF YOU EMAIL AN AUTHOR OR LEADER OR CONTACT THEM THROUGH FACEBOOK OR ANOTHER SOCIAL SITE, BE POLITE, RESPECTFUL, AND SPECIFIC. Not only are these folks reading your note, but they are also probably reading many others. The most popular authors may receive upwards of fifty emails or messages *every day*. If you have questions, try and be specific. I am often contacted by Pagans who want me to help them find their path or learn more about Witchcraft. That's a pretty broad request and not one I can really help with, beyond suggesting a few good books. On the other hand, when people have specific questions, I do try and answer them. Never be nasty or impatient, even if someone doesn't write you back or gives you an answer you don't like. As I said, these are very busy folks, and most of them already spend as much time as they possibly can helping the Pagan community.

Pass it along. If people are helpful to you as you walk your path, once you are more experienced and newer Witches come to you for answers, try and take the time to help them out. That's the way it works. People taught me. I pass on my knowledge to you. You pass it on to the next Witch. We all help each other learn and grow to the best of our individual abilities.

One last note, if you are contacting a Pagan author—*Never, ever, ever* send an author a copy of the book you are working on unless they specifically request that you do so. (Which they probably won't.) This is a pretty common request: "I'm working on a great book on—insert topic here—and I'd like you to take a look at it. I know you'll love it. Then could you please help me get the book published?" Published authors can't look at unpublished work for a number of reasons, including legal issues and a simple lack of time. If you have an established relationship with an author, they may be willing to take a look, but otherwise, please don't even ask. Some authors will be happy to talk to you about writing in general, or your work in particular, but again—be polite if they feel they have to say no.

Besides finding Witches who live near you or contacting other Pagans online, there is another option for meeting up with others of like mind: festivals and conventions.

There are a number of large and small Pagan gatherings that are held every year. Some of these are huge, with thousands of people from all different paths coming from far and wide. Others are small and mostly limited to folks from the local region. Many areas have Pagan Pride Day celebrations that also welcome non-Pagans or curious seekers in the name of openness and education.

Before you decide to go to a gathering, there are a few factors you should consider:

How far are you willing to travel? Some of the biggest festivals may be far away from where you live. If you don't like to travel, you may want to start with something smaller and closer and see if you like it enough to make traveling to a larger more distant one worthwhile.

How much are you willing to spend? Since this book is all about *not* spending money, you should consider the difference between a small event, which may be free or cost just a few dollars, and a larger one, which can cost you hundreds (or more) by the time you are through paying for travel expenses, hotels, food, and entrance fees.

Are there ways to cut costs and make a more expensive event affordable? For instance, some festivals have camping as an option, which is much cheaper than paying for a hotel room (and the camping may be included in the entry fee). Can you share a room with one or more people? Do you have a friend who lives nearby with whom you can stay? Can you drive instead of fly? All these are issues to take into consideration when making your decision.

If you are an artist or a craftsperson, do you want to sell your items at the event? Many festivals have the option to be a vendor. If you have Pagan items to sell, you might be able to at least pay for the cost of attending, or even make extra money. Of course, you won't be free to enjoy as much of the activities as you would if you weren't vending.

HOW BIG A CROWD CAN YOU HANDLE? This is an important question. Pagans, as a rule, tend to be fairly sensitive people. Not all of us are up to dealing with crowds, especially when those crowds number in the thousands. Be realistic about your own ability to cope with the masses, and if this can be an issue for you, you might want to start off by trying a small event and working your way up to larger ones. (I am not particularly comfortable with large groups, but thankfully, large groups of Pagans don't seem to bother me as much. You may discover you are the same.)

ARE YOU PLANNING ON BRINGING CHILDREN? Not every Pagan gathering is equally child-friendly. Some of the larger outdoor events are "clothing optional." Not all parents want their children to see naked strangers, and not all children would be comfortable in that situation. If you are not certain if the event you are considering attending is appropriate for your children, it is best to contact the event coordinators and find out for sure. In addition, not all events are open to children, so double-check before going.

DO YOU HAVE ANY SPECIAL MEDICAL ISSUES? Not all outdoor events are handicapped accessible or easy to get around at. If there is a ritual, you may be expected to stand for a long period of time. (People with issues are almost always accommodated, but if the coordinators don't know ahead of time, they may not anticipate a problem. And if you need to sit, you might have to bring your own chair and be willing to sit outside the circle if others need to move around. It pays to plan ahead.)

ARE YOU WILLING TO VOLUNTEER? Some festivals will give you a price break (or let you attend for free) if you are willing to help out. It is worth looking into. Volunteering is also a good way to get to know people and give back to the community.

WHAT DO YOU WANT TO GET OUT OF THE EVENT AND HOW MUCH IS IT WORTH TO YOU? This is the biggest question you should ask yourself before making plans to attend a festival or gathering. Whether something is a bargain or not is not just based on what you pay for it, but also on what you get out of the event in return. For instance, if you want to attend a ritual at Samhain, you can probably find one that is free or relatively cheap. If you want to take lots of interesting classes and workshops, meet Pagan authors, and take part in varied rituals, you will need to consider a much larger festival that will certainly cost more money. If you just want to meet other Witches and you don't care about much else, you should probably be able to find some kind of event that won't cost you an arm and a leg, but you may have to travel a bit to do it. Figure out what you are looking for and how much money you can spend to get it. Then, take a look around to see if you can find an event that will satisfy your needs without breaking your budget.

Once you have figured out which type of event you would like to attend, you can look at the options and make an informed decision. Pagan events are often advertised in various Witchcraft magazines and can also be found online. They usually fall around the same time each year, so you can start clearing your schedule way in advance. For instance, Circle Sanctuary's huge yearly event, Pagan Spirit Gathering (Missouri), is always held for a week around the Summer Solstice.

Whether you travel the country meeting up with other Witches, spend hours chatting on Facebook and looking up information online, or simply sit in the comfort of your own living room and read book after book, you will undoubtedly spend some money on your pursuit of knowledge. How much you spend is up to you—especially now that you know about all the possibilities.

But keep in mind that Witches have always relied on each other to keep our wisdom alive and growing. Even during the years when magick had to hide its face, there were brave and dedicated people who worked to ensure that our traditions survived.

Let us hope that such dark days will never come again. But in the meanwhile, we still struggle to find the learning we desire and to help non-Pagans understand who we really are and what we believe in.

My point is this: whenever possible, share your knowledge. I'm not saying you should go up to people on the street and start telling them all about Witchcraft. But when you have the opportunity to pass your hard-earned learning on to others, take the time and energy to do so.

In this way, we preserve the lessons we have learned and help others to learn and grow as well. As individuals and as a community, knowledge is power—so let's do all we can to increase our power as Witches together.

DEBORAH'S PERSONAL LIBRARY

For those of you just starting out and trying to decide which books are worth spending your hard-earned cash on, here is a partial list of some of my favorites (note that while I have divided them into general categories for ease of use, many of them actually overlap or cover more than one area). Some of these are readily available classics, and some are more obscure—and this is by no means a complete list of my personal Pagan library. For instance, I haven't put in any of my many books on tarot, runes, or astrology. Or cat magick. But it will at least give you a starting point, as well as a list of books to keep your eyes open for when you are pursuing the many avenues discussed earlier. Naturally, my own books are on the list, too!

Witchcraft Basics:

Blake, Deborah. *The Everyday Witch A to Z: An Amusing, Inspiring & Informative Guide to the Wonderful World of Witchcraft.* St. Paul: Llewellyn, 2012.

Buckland, Raymond. *Buckland's Complete Book of Witchcraft.* St. Paul: Llewellyn, 2002.

—. *Wicca for Life: The Way of the Craft—from Birth to Summerland.* New York: Citadel Press, 2018.

Cunningham, Scott. *Wicca: A Guide for the Solitary Practitioner.* St. Paul: Llewellyn, 2010.

Dubats, Sally. *Natural Magick.* New York: Citadel, 2002.

Grimassi, Raven. *Spirit of the Witch: Religion & Spirituality in Contemporary Witchcraft.* St. Paul: Llewellyn, 2003.

Holland, Eileen. *The Wicca Handbook.* York Beach: Weiser Books, 2008.

McCoy, Edain. *The Witch's Coven: Finding or Forming Your Own Circle.* St. Paul: Llewellyn, 1997

Seville, Christine. *Practical Wicca the Easy Way: Spells and Rituals to Heal and Harmonize Your Life.* New York: Sterling Publishing Company, 2003.

Trobe, Kala. *The Witch's Guide to Life.* St. Paul: Llewellyn, 2003.

Tuitean, Paul, and Estelle Daniels. *Pocket Guide to Wicca.* Freedom: The Crossing Press, 1998.

Herbs:

Cunningham, Scott. *The Complete Book of Incense, Oils & Brews*. St. Paul: Llewellyn, 2002.

—. *Cunningham's Encyclopedia of Magical Herbs*. St. Paul: Llewellyn, 2012.

—. *Magical Herbalism*. St. Paul: Llewellyn, 1986.

Dugan, Ellen. *Cottage Witchery: Natural Magick for Hearth and Home*. St. Paul: Llewellyn, 2012.

—. *Garden Witchery: Magick from the Ground Up*. St. Paul: Llewellyn, 2013.

Dunwich, Gerina. *The Wicca Garden: A Modern Witch's Book of Magickal and Enchanted Herbs and Plants*. New York: Citadel Press, 2018.

Morrison, Dorothy. *Bud, Blossom, & Leaf: The Magical Herb Gardener's Handbook*. Chicago: Crossed Crow Books, 2024.

Roth, Harold. *The Witching Herbs: 13 Essential Plants and Herbs for Your Magical Garden*. Newburyport: Weiser Books, 2017.

Gemstones:

Chase, Pamela Louise, and Jonathan Pawlik. *Healing with Gemstones*. Franklin Lakes: New Page, 2002.

Cunningham, Scott. *Cunningham's Encyclopedia of Crystal, Gem & Metal Magic*. St. Paul: Llewellyn, 2011.

Rituals & Spellcasting:

Barrette, Elizabeth. *Composing Magic: How to Create Magical Spells, Rituals, Blessings, Chants, and Prayers*. Newberryport: Weiser, 2007.

Blake, Deborah. *Circle, Coven & Grove: A Year of Magickal Practice*. Chicago: Crossed Crow Books, 2023.

—. *Everyday Witch A to Z Spellbook: Wonderfully Witchy Blessing, Charms & Spells.* St. Paul: Llewellyn, 2010.

Connor, Kerri. *The Pocket Spell Creator: Magickal References at Your Fingertips.* Franklin Lakes: New Page Books, 2003.

Dugan, Ellen. *The Enchanted Cat: Feline Fascinations, Spells & Magick.* St. Paul: Llewellyn, 2012.

Galenorn, Yasmine. *Embracing the Moon: A Witch's Guide to Ritual Spellcraft and Shadow Work.* Kirkland: Nightqueen Enterprises LLC, 2015.

Hardie, Titania. *Titania's Magical Compendium: Spells and Rituals to Bring a Little Magic into Your Life.* San Diego: Thunder Bay Press, 2003.

Johnstone, Michael. *The Ultimate Encyclopedia of Spells.* New York: Gramercy Books, 2004.

Nahmad, Claire. *Catspells: A Collection of Enchantments for You and Your Feline Companion.* Philadelphia: Running Press, 1993.

Renee, Janina. *By Candlelight: Rites for Celebration, Blessing & Prayer.* St. Paul: Llewellyn, 2004.

Telesco, Patricia. *Your Book of Shadows: How to Write Your Own Magickal Spells.* New York: Citadel Press, 1999.

West, Kate. *The Real Witches' Year: Spells, Rituals and Meditations for Every Day of the Year.* London: Element, 2004.

Wood, Gail. *Rituals of the Dark Moon: 13 Lunar Rites for a Magical Path.* St. Paul: Llewellyn, 2004.

Sabbats & Lunar Lore:

Cole, Jennifer. *Ceremonies of the Seasons: Exploring and Celebrating Nature's Eternal Cycle.* London: Duncan Baird Publishers, 2007.

Dunwich, Gerina. *The Pagan Book of Halloween: A Complete Guide to the Magick, Incantations, Recipes, Spells and Lore.* New York: Penguin Compass, 2000.

Green, Marian. *A Witch Alone: The Essential Guide foir the Solo Practitioner of the Magical Arts.* Newburyport: Hampton Roads Publishing, 2009.

Kynes, Sandra. *Witches' Sabbats & Esbats.* Chicago: Crossed Crow Books, 2023.

Morrison, Dorothy. *Everyday Moon Magic.* St. Paul: Llewellyn, 2012.

Ravenwolf, Silver. *Halloween: Customs, Recipes, & Spells.* St. Paul: Llewellyn, 1999.

History, Classics & Traditional Practices:

Adler, Margot. *Drawing Down the Moon: Witches, Druids, Goddess-Worshippers, and Other Pagans in America Today.* New York: Penguin, 2006.

Fitch, Ed. *Magical Rites from the Crystal Well: A Classic Text for Witches & Pagans.* St. Paul: Llewellyn, 1984.

Starhawk. *The Spiral Dance: A Rebirth of the Ancient Religion of the Great Goddess.* San Francisco: Harper-SanFrancisco, 1999.

Telesco, Patricia, Editor. *Cakes and Ale for the Pagan Soul: Spells, Recipes, and Reflections from NeoPagan Elders and Teachers.* Berkley: The Crossing Press, 2005.

Wildman, Laura, Editor. *Celebrating the Pagan Soul: Our Own Stories of Inspiration and Community.* New York: Citadel Books, 2005.

Gods & Goddesses:

Bolen, Jean Shinoda. *Goddesses in Older Women: Archetypes in Women Over Fifty.* NY: Harper Paperbacks, 2014.

Jordan, Michael. *Encyclopedia of Gods: Over 2,500 Deities of the World.* Brattleboro: Echo Point Books & Media, 2022.

Wood, Gail. *The Wild God: Rituals and Meditations on the Sacred Masculine.* Niceville: Spilled Candy Books, 2006.

Personal Practices:

Ardinger, Barbara. *Pagan Every Day: Finding the Extraordinary in Our Ordinary Lives*. San Francisco: Red Wheel/Weiser, 2006.

Blake, Deborah. *The Goddess is in the Detail: Wisdom for the Everyday Witch*. St. Paul: Llewellyn, 2009.

Curott, Phyllis. *Book of Shadows: A Modern Woman's Journey into the Wisdom of Witchcraft and the Magic of the Goddess*. New York: Harmony Books, 1999.

Digitalis, Raven. *Shadow Magick Compendium*. Chicago: Crossed Crow Books, 2022.

Dubats, Sally. *Natural Magick: The Essential Witch's Grimoire*. New York: Citadel Press, 2002.

Dumars, Denise. *Be Blessed: Daily Devotions for Busy Wiccans and Pagans*. Franklin Lakes: New Page, 2006.

Eilers, Dana D. *The Practical Pagan: Commonsense Guidelines for Modern Practitioners*. Franklin Lakes: New Page, 2002.

Henes, Donna. *The Queen of My Self: Stepping into Sovereignty in Midlife*. Brooklyn: Monarch Press, 2005.

Moura, Ann. *Green Witchcraft: Folk Magic, Fairy Lore & Herb Craft*. St. Paul: Llewellyn, 2014.

Singer, Marion. *A Witch's 10 Commandments: Magickal Guidelines for Everyday Life*. New York: Simon & Schuster, 2006.

Sylvan, Dianne. *The Circle Within: Creating a Wiccan Spiritual Tradition*. St. Paul: Llewellyn, 2012.

Weinstein, Marion. *Positive Magic: Occult Self-Help*. Newburyport: Weiser Books, 2020.

Correspondences & Reference:

Greer, John Michael. *The New Encyclopedia of the Occult*. St. Paul: Llewellyn, 2003.

Grimassi, Raven. *Encyclopedia of Wicca and Witchcraft*. St. Paul: Llewellyn, 2000.

Guiley, Rosemary Ellen. *The Encyclopedia of Magic and Alchemy.* New York: Checkmark Books, 2006.

—. *The Encyclopedia of Witches & Witchcraft: Second Edition.* New York: Checkmark Books, 1999.

Holland, Eileen. *Holland's Grimoire of Magickal Correspondences: A Ritual Handbook.* Franklin Lakes: Red Wheel/Weiser, 2005.

Illes, Judika. *The Element Encyclopedia of Witchcraft.* Hammersmith: Harper Element, 2014.

McColman, Carl. *The Well-Read Witch: Essential Books for Your Magickal Library.* Franklin Lakes: New Page Books, 2002.

Rosean, Lexa. The Encyclopedia of Magickal Ingredients: A Wiccan Guide to Spellcasting. New York: Pocket Books, 2005.

Advanced Learning:

Bonewits, Isaac. *Real Magic: An Introductory Treatise on the Basic Principles of Yellow Magic.* Boston: Samuel Weiser, 1989.

Cunningham, Scott. *Earth, Air, Fire & Water: More Techniques of Natural Magic.* St. Paul: Llewellyn, 2012.

—. *Living Wicca: A Further Guide for the Solitary Practitioner.* St. Paul: Llewellyn, 2012.

De Angeles, Ly. *Witchcraft Theory and Practice.* St. Paul: Llewellyn, 2012.

McCoy, Edain. *Spellworking for Covens: Magick for Two or More.* St. Paul: Llewellyn, 2002.

Penczak, Christopher. *The Mystic Foundation: Understanding & Exploring the Magical Universe.* St. Paul: Llewellyn, 2006.

Telesco, Patricia. *Advanced Wicca: Exploring Deeper Levels of Spiritual Skills and Masterful Magick.* New York: Citadel Press, 2000.

Weinstein, Marion. *Earth Magic: A Book of Shadows for Positive Witches.* Franklin Lakes: New Page Books, 2003.

In addition: I subscribe to a number of Pagan magazines, including *Sage Woman* and *Witches and Pagans,* both from BBI Media.

Chapter 3

The Economical Home: Creating and Maintaining Sacred Space

A Witch's home is their castle. And often, also their temple and place of worship. But most of us don't have the money to live like kings. So how can we combine the mundane and the sacred, put our own particular witchy touch on our surroundings, and still have enough money to turn on the lights? (Candles are nice for rituals, but you wouldn't want to live with them all the time.)

The Altar

Let's start in the center of the Witch's home—the altar. Now obviously, your altar doesn't have to be in the middle of your house or apartment; but regardless of its location, for many of us, our altar is the spiritual core of our living space.

Whether it is large or small, ornate or plain, the altar is where we go to cast spells, talk to the gods, or merely light a stick of our favorite incense. It is not only a physical manifestation of our beliefs; it is in many ways a window into our souls.

No small task, then, to create the perfect altar. Luckily, it only has to be perfect for one person—you. Even better, it doesn't have to take a lot of money to create this spiritual center for your home. You can even have more than one if you desire. (I have two, for instance: my original altar in my bedroom and a newer addition in my dining room/ writing space.) You just need to decide what you want and the cheapest way to achieve it!

Step One: Location, Location, Location

Where you put your altar can be almost as important as what you put on it. If you share your space with others (especially non-Witch others), you'll want to be sure to place your altar where you can use it in privacy. This will probably mean devoting a corner of your bedroom to altar space if you don't have a spare room you can use for this purpose. But if you need a private spot and don't have one, you can try using a screen to divide your spiritual space off from the rest of the house. A cheap screen can be fashioned from three panels of old shutters hinged together. You can paint the shutters a glossy black or cover them with magickal designs if you are more artistic. Or you can build a screen with inexpensive frames made out of molding with fabric stapled over the edges. (A staple gun is a handy tool and usually costs less than ten dollars.) Check the discount fabric by-the-yard bin at your local Walmart or look for remnants at a fabric store. A twin-sized bedspread or throw can also be a colorful screen, or you can hang one on the wall behind your altar to mark off the area.

Step Two: Build a Base

Most people use some kind of table for the base of their altars, but an altar can be any piece of furniture that will hold your sacred items. The altar in my bedroom, for instance, is an unfinished wooden shelf purchased from a local store for about ten dollars. (It was cheap in part because it was designed to be painted over, but I decided that I preferred the look of the raw wood, so I left it that way.) I simply screwed it to the wall, wound a blue scarf with stars on it through the wooden rungs at the front of the shelf to dress it up a bit, and placed my magickal items on it. Voila—instant altar. (And the scarf was free: a hand-me-down from a friend when she moved and no longer had a use for it.) The shelf has the added advantage of being high enough on the wall to put it out of the reach of my many cats; thus making it safe to leave candles burning, place flowers where Magic the Cat won't find and steal them, and leave any magickal items made of string, herbs, or other materials that might prove too much of a temptation if left at table-jumping level.

On the other hand, my second altar is both fancier and more expensive. The flat surface is the top of what was designed to be a bed-side table, with a closed cabinet and a drawer underneath made of polished oak. I store many of my magickal supplies in the cabinet, my candles in the drawer, and use the top to hold a bowl of stones, some other ritual items, and whatever spell I am working on at the moment. On the wall above, I have a beautiful wooden cabinet made by one of the woodworkers at the artists' cooperative shop I run. The glass door reveals neat rows of homemade magickal oils, various hunks of gemstones, bags of runes, my containers for salt and water, and other smaller ritual tools. On the top of the cabinet, I have other esoteric items as well.

When I got around to creating this second altar, I decided I wanted something more complicated (and more multi-purpose) than my first altar, and that I was willing to spend a bit more money to have exactly what I wanted. Part of being frugal is deciding *where* to put what money you are going to spend. And I bartered work time for part of the cost of the cabinet to make it fit in my budget. Never underestimate the possibilities of barter!

You need to make sure your altar space fits your needs. (I loved my first altar, but I realized eventually that my magickal supplies had seriously outgrown the original space, and I was tired of just tucking them into miscellaneous cupboards and then not being able to find them when I needed them.)

So, before you set out to create your altar space, think about how you are going to use it. Do you just want a flat surface to place a few items on or something that can store all your tools, supplies, etc.? Does it need to be tucked away in a corner, or can it be out where you can look at it and use it every day? Do you want to keep your magickal books with your ritual tools? What height works best for the magickal work you will be doing at your altar? Does it need to be out of the reach of pets or toddlers? Do you want something fancy or something plain and simple? Once you have answered these questions, you can decide whether or not any of these inexpensive options might be a good choice for your altar base—just make sure they're steady enough not to fall over and spill your lit candle or carefully crafted oils onto the floor.

FOR A SMALL ALTAR:

- A tray table or an old tray placed on top of a crate or sturdy metal plant stand. Old trays can usually be found at yard sales, second-hand stores, and elderly relatives' houses, and they can be decoupaged with Pagan symbols if you want to make them look more witchy.

- A large wooden crate placed on end. You can store some things underneath in the crate itself and cover the opening with a cloth if you want to.
- Stack two plastic milk crates together (if you want them to be steadier, you can tie or duct tape them together), and cover with a pretty cloth.
- An old metal plant stand will work if it is big enough and has enough level and flat space on top.

FOR A LARGER ALTAR:

- Place an old door across two file cabinets, sturdy wood crates, or any other tallish boxes or cabinets of equal height. Cover with a cloth or use bottom sections for storage or display.
- Old steamer trunks or newer travel trunks make great altars, with or without a cloth to disguise them. These can often be picked up at yard sales or second-hand stores for relatively small amounts, or you might still have one kicking around from college. I recently inherited an old trunk that my grandmother's parents came over from Russia with—some good family vibes never hurt when considering a piece for your altar. And less commonly used ritual items can be stored inside if it isn't too inconvenient when you actually need to get to them.
- Shelf units will work as altars, too. Pick the shelf that is at the best height for your main working altar, and then use the other shelves for your magickal books, supplies, or as a display for your statuary and crystals. Shelf units can vary in size, shape, color, and composition. A black metal shelf may work well for a Goth

Witch, for instance, whereas a Green Witch may prefer one made out of natural wood. Cheap shelf units can be found at yard sales, discount stores, and sometimes even abandoned on the curb. Keep your eyes open for one which might work for you. It might even be sitting in your garage or basement right now, gathering dust!

- Small tables, such as those designed to hold little television sets or go by the bedside are often perfect for altars. Look in junk stores, used furniture stores, and even old furniture/antique stores for something funky and functional.

- Old desks, dressers, and dining room tables can be used if they are small enough or your space is large enough. Cover them with a pretty cloth or bedspread, or paint them a glossy black, red, or metallic color.

- If you are handy, you can build yourself a simple altar out of scrap lumber. Sometimes lumber yards will sell you left-over bits and pieces for virtually nothing. With a hammer and a few nails, a little paint, you can create an altar in almost any size and shape that suits your needs. (And this kind of carpentry is pretty simple—even I can do it, and I'm a lousy nailer.)

In truth, an altar can be made from almost anything, depending on what you are willing to spend and how you want to use it. With a little imagination, you can find, reinvent, or build yourself the perfect altar. Of course, then you have to figure out what to put on it.

Step Three: Design Your Altar Setup

There is no hard and fast rule about which magickal items you should have on your altar, and no two Witches' altars are alike. You can find plenty of suggestions for altar set-ups in any of the standard "Introduction to Witchcraft" books. None of them will be alike, either, in all likelihood.

The simplest altar may have nothing more than a pretty cloth and a candle. More formal altars may have dozens of items, arranged precisely according to the beliefs and requirements of that particular Witch's magickal path. Your altar should reflect your beliefs, your priorities, and your own personality. Let's face it: if you are a neat person, you will probably want an organized and tidy altar space. If you're…let's say…more relaxed about things, you will probably end up with a surface that is covered with odds and ends that have struck your fancy at one time or another. There is no right or wrong way to do it—just follow your heart.

The only real "rule," if there is one, is to keep your altar space free of non-magickal clutter and clean it occasionally. After all, anything less would be disrespectful to the gods, and nobody wants that.

So, what should you put on your altar? Here is a list of some of the more commonly used items:

GODDESS AND/OR GOD STATUES.

ONE CANDLE EACH FOR THE GODDESS AND GOD, often in fancy candle holders. Some people use metallic silver and gold candles or cream and yellow.

CANDLES FOR EACH OF THE FOUR QUARTERS—usually green or brown for North (Earth), yellow for East (Air), red for South (Fire), and blue for West (Water). These are often smaller than the Goddess and God candles. An inexpensive choice is to use what are called "chime" candles; a mini candle that usually cost around a dollar each. (You can find these at Pagan or New Age stores and online.) These candles also have their own holders.

INCENSE AND AN INCENSE HOLDER. Incense holders can be very simple or extremely ornate (I've seen dragon-shaped holders that are fashioned so that the smoke from the incense comes out the dragon's nostrils. Very cool.) The incense itself can vary from quite cheap (the dollar store often has some…but I can't vouch for how it smells) to more expensive options made from essential oils or exotic herbs. I use incense made from essential oils because I'm allergic to most other incense, but you don't have to spend much money on incense if you don't want to. There are lots of specialty incenses made especially for magickal use—for the most part, you can skip these and merely bless your own inexpensive incense as needed.

CRYSTALS OF VARIOUS TYPES. Lots of Witches like to use gemstones and crystals in their magickal work, myself included. Because they come from the Earth, they can be quite powerful, and many folks believe that each different type of stone has a special vibration that makes it particularly useful for a particular magickal task—lapis for healing or rose quartz for love, for example. I have a large crystal quartz that I use during Full Moon rituals and for any healing work I do. And I confess, I am something of a gemstone junkie (I'm also a jewelry maker, which might have something to do with it), and have collected quite a few impressive specimens over the years. The drawback to crystals and other gemstones is that they can be quite expensive, especially in larger sizes. However, there is nothing that says you have to use a gigantic three-foot amethyst crystal—a small, tumbled amethyst stone can often be just as effective and cost only a dollar or two. I've also gotten large lots of tumbled stones and crystals on eBay for five or ten dollars plus shipping. If you have some Witchy friends, you can even split the price and divide the lot up between you.

SALT AND WATER. Many Witches use a mixture of salt and water in their rituals for purification and consecration. Sea salt is most commonly used and is fairly inexpensive, but you can always use plain table salt instead. Water, obviously, is free, although many folks collect water from streams, oceans, rain, or other natural sources rather than using water from the tap. The salt and water are often in special containers, some of which can also be quite fancy. Try looking in second-hand stores or stores that carry hand-crafted items—you can probably find small, unique containers for next to nothing. If you want a small dish to mix the salt and water in, a tiny piece of pottery or a curved seashell work well.

A CHALICE. The chalice symbolizes the womb of the Goddess and everything female and can be made of wood, metal, pottery, or glass. (I don't advise plastic, although I suppose you could use that as well.) There are many truly beautiful—and truly expensive—chalices available from Pagan shops; I've seen ones that cost fifty dollars or even more. And if you have the money to spend, and one of these captures your heart, by all means, go ahead and get it. On the other hand, I have some really nice handmade pottery goblets, some of which cost me around ten dollars. This is a good item to look for at craft shows where pottery is often very reasonably priced. (Or at a shop that features handmade work by local artisans and crafters, like the one I run.) You can often also find old metal cups and goblets at second-hand stores for next to nothing.

AN ATHAME. The athame is the Witch's ritual knife and symbolizes the God and the masculine. Again, these can vary from simple and inexpensive wood models to ornate and very pricy silver decorated with gemstones. The simple one works just as well as the fancy one, so which you end up with is a matter of taste and budget.

A DRUM. Or six. Many Witches use drums and other musical instruments, including rattles and flutes. If you want, you can make your own drum quite easily from an old coffee can, or a rattle from an empty jar filled with popcorn kernels.

FLOWERS IN A VASE. Flowers are often used to decorate the altar and as an offering to the gods. The cheapest way to do this, obviously, is to grow your own flowers in your yard, garden, or an inside pot and then pick one or two as needed. You can also pick wildflowers during the warmer months, as long as you are not on private land, and you are certain the flowers you're picking aren't endangered. Many weeds actually have very pretty flowers and grow in such abundance that the two or three you take for your altar will never be missed. And you don't need to use a fancy vase, either. I assure you, the Goddess doesn't care if you use a vase you got at the dollar store or picked up at a yard sale. And all sorts of miscellaneous items found around the home can serve as vases including mugs, empty jars, and even fancy shampoo or perfume bottles once you're through with their original contents.

ANYTHING ELSE THAT HAS MEANING TO YOU. Some Witches keep their Book of Shadows on their altar, or a piece of paper with their current spell on it. Others put pictures of those they love, people and pets they have lost, or something that symbolizes whatever goal they are working toward.

I've talked a little bit about some less expensive options for altar items, and in the next chapter, I'll go into even more detail on possible substitutions. But keep in mind that there are many wonderful and magickal things that can be found in nature, and depending on where you live, picked up off the ground for free. Try using some of the following on your altar, either instead of or in addition to the items mentioned above.

- Shells
- Stones (these don't have to be gemstones—lots of rocks have a natural beauty while having no monetary value whatsoever, and river stones can be particularly pretty.)
- Feathers (keeping in mind that it is illegal to own eagle feathers and those of some other endangered species.)
- Leaves—especially in the fall when they change colors.
- Pinecones
- Beach glass (this is glass that has been tumbled by the waves.)
- Dried flowers
- Herbs—both fresh and dried (many herbs have lovely flowers, too.)
- Fresh flowers
- Acorns
- Snake skins—snakes often shed their skins and leave them behind mostly intact. Snakes are a symbol of change, growth, and rebirth, so if you are doing magickal work involving these elements, a snakeskin might be a good thing to put on your altar (unless snakes freak you out, of course).
- Antlers—at certain times of the year, you can sometimes find antlers that have been shed by

> deer (or other animals, depending on where you live).
- Bird's nests—once the birds are through using them, you can often find compact and intricate nests.

Of course, any and all of the objects can also be placed anywhere around the rest of the house, giving it a magickal and earthy Pagan feel.

THE MAGICKAL HOME

The altar may be the center of the Witch's home, but that doesn't mean it has to be the only part of the house that reflects your witchy spirit and lifestyle. Most of us have some touches of our magickal paths scattered throughout our living space, even if they are as subtle as nature photos and a few scattered rocks instead of a giant pentacle in the middle of the dining room table. (I've got a large pentacle candle holder with stained glass on my table, actually, made by one of my circle-mates. Beautiful. But I live by myself, so I can decorate any way I want to.)

Inexpensive ways to give your home a Pagan feel include using any of the natural objects listed above, as well as many homemade crafts (some of which are found in Chapter Five). You can also hang funky posters in cheap frames (try *overstockArt.com* for a mundane source of artwork—there is enough variety on this site, you are certain to find something with a witchy bent) or pin a cool printed tapestry or bedspread to the wall.

Here are a few more basic decorating tips to make your home feel like a castle, even if you can't afford to live in one:

USE MIRRORS TO MAKE ANY SPACE SEEM LARGER. This works particularly well in small rooms. If you don't want to spend the money on large mirrors, you can find used ones (sometimes the glass is old and wavy, which gives it a Gothic look) or use mirrored tiles with double stick tape on the back. For a magickal boost, place a mirror behind your altar to reflect your spells out into the universe.

PAINT IS A CHEAP WAY TO CHANGE THE WAY A ROOM LOOKS. Traditionally, white or light-colored paint is used to make a room look larger and airier, but you can use any color you like to create a mood or feeling. For instance, if you like the feel of the ocean, you can paint a space with greens and blues. If you are more of the dark and Goth inclination, glossy black, steel gray, or bright red might be more your style. You aren't limited to painting the walls, either. You can paint the ceiling (try something dark, then add silver cut-out stars), the furniture, or even a large ceramic flowerpot. For an extra touch, you can paint magickal symbols, sigils, or messages on the wall underneath your layers of paint. Paint can even be charged with protective properties to help keep you, your home, and your family safe. Your only limit is the power of your imagination (and your landlord, in some cases—keep in mind that dark paints can be tough to cover up later if you don't own the place you live).

COLLECTIONS OF LIKE-OBJECTS GROUPED TOGETHER CAN BE VERY STRIKING WITHOUT HAVING TO COST MUCH. Try putting together a collection (like dragons, cats, or Witch figurines), or gather a number of pieces that are all the same color (like a vase, a statue, a drum, and a wooden box, all in bright red). This is especially fun to do with miscellaneous bits and pieces that you gather in your travels or items that have a particular spiritual meaning to you. I collect rocks from everywhere I go, for instance. Individually, they're just rocks. But together, they look quite impressive, give a natural feel to a room, and contain the essence of every place I've traveled.

Create your own monograms or write words on pillows, wall hangings, or framed pieces of cloth using iron-on appliqué letters that can be found at fabric or craft stores. Or use fabric paints and stencils to do the same thing. Try using words like "joy," "peace," or "magick," as daily reminders of what you are trying to achieve.

Buy a cheap frame and use it to dress up a black-and-white photo (take the picture yourself to be really frugal and use your computer to turn it into a stark black-and-white piece of art). Or if you are the crafty type, stitch up a witchy saying in needlepoint and frame that. I know a woman who has a beautiful, embroidered sampler of the Wiccan Rede that she made herself—it is a beautiful thing to behold.

Use high-gloss paint to dress up everyday objects. A plain old metal shelf can be quite striking if you paint it a glossy black or a vibrant crimson. This is especially nice for your magickal tools if you want to set them off from the rest of your belongings.

Use shelves to organize your clutter or show off your collections (or both). And for books, of course. Instead of expensive built-in bookshelves, try using utility shelves. They can be ugly, but you can dress them up with paint (as mentioned above) or hang decorative cloth off the sides to hide the not-so-pretty bits. Or find used shelves at yard sales, used furniture stores, and going-out-of-business sales. Many store display shelves can look quite nice in a house and be useful as well. Keep your magickal books separate from the mundane ones on a plain wooden bookshelf that you've decorated with shells, dried leaves, or witchy symbols.

TO BRING THE LOOK OF NATURE INSIDE, YOU CAN COVER ONE WALL WITH A WALL-SIZED POSTER OF A BEACH, THE DESERT, OR MOUNTAINS. Try *muralsyourway.com* (Environmental Graphics) to buy one that is premade, or have one made up from your own picture. Obviously, a poster that size isn't cheap, but if you live in the city (or a place with few windows) and want to surround yourself with a bit of the natural world, it can be a good investment. Just make sure to pick something you won't get tired of looking at every day!

FOR A CHEAPER ALTERNATIVE, IF YOU HAVE AN ARTISTIC BENT, YOU CAN PAINT A MURAL ON ONE WALL. My brother-in-law is an amazing artist, and he made one entire wall in their living room into a beach scene. There's another wall that looks like an old castle. If you're lucky enough to have talent (or talented friends), you can create any kind of atmosphere you want. And don't forget the barter system. If you know someone with artistic abilities, maybe you can work out an exchange that doesn't involve money. (If you can cook well, for instance, you can offer meals for a month. If you are good at something, there is often someone else who isn't and might be willing to trade.)

MOOD LIGHTING. One of the easiest ways to create a mood is with lighting. This doesn't have to be expensive, either. Candles are a fairly cheap way to create a soothing or mystical aura, of course, but you can also use a lamp with a dimmer switch (they make ones you can add to existing lamps, so you don't have to pay for an electrician to come over and add a special switch to the wall), or simply throw a filmy cloth over the top of a lamp (making sure the cloth won't get too hot, of course).

Fabric can change the look of a room in other ways as well. To add texture and interest, staple burlap to the walls (it can be dyed in various colors and may even be cheaper than paint—certainly, it is easier to change), hang mosquito netting or flowing curtains from the ceiling over your bed, or drape a silky cloth over the sofa. Fabric doesn't have to be expensive to look beautiful, and you can often find remnants for next to nothing at fabric stores. You can also "reinvent" old sheets, curtains, bedspreads, and other cloth items by turning them into pillows, couch covers, wall hangings, or room dividers. Small pieces of fabric can be sewn together to make larger ones and even old clothing can be turned into something new and decorative for the house. I once recovered my sofa using nothing but a pair of sheets and a few yards of inexpensive trim. If you can find fabrics with witchy themes, like moons or stars, they can convert a mundane room into a magickal refuge from the rest of the world.

Use one large object as the focal point of the room. Sometimes if you have one special piece (whether you spent a lot of money on it or just found it somewhere), it is enough to make the room seem special even when all the rest of the furniture in it is nothing major.

Create balance with pairs of things: shelf units on either side of a television, for example, or candlesticks on either end of a mantle. This kind of balancing act makes a room look orderly and well put together, even when all the pieces in it are plain or inexpensive.

Decorating your home doesn't have to be expensive or complicated; the trick is to figure out what kind of style you like and use simple techniques like the ones above to achieve it without spending too much money. And you don't have to buy out the local Pagan store to get a magickal home, either—simply use your imagination and a little extra time and energy to create a place where you can feel like a king. Or queen, of course.

A note on maintaining the sacred space of your home:

It is hard for the place you live in to feel like a refuge from the world outside if it is dirty and cluttered. Both physical messes and stagnant or negative energy can turn sacred space into a depressing, distracting, and unpleasant environment. And nobody wants that. But we are all busy folks, and it is not unusual to let things like tidying up the living room or clearing the space after a fight with your significant other slide to the bottom of the priority list. I fight this battle just like everybody else, of course. And here are a few of the techniques I have found helpful over the years—maybe you will find them helpful as well.

DO A LITTLE BIT EVERY DAY, AND AS MUCH AS POSSIBLE, CLEAN UP AS YOU GO. This is the number-one easiest way to ease the burden of cleaning and neatening your home. Once the housecleaning jobs get too big, they are overwhelming. If you spent even fifteen minutes every day neatening up: putting away the laundry, filing paperwork, or vacuuming, for instance, you will find that you have accomplished many of the chores with very little effort.

SET ASIDE AN HOUR OR TWO EVERY WEEK TO TACKLE THE BIGGER JOBS, THEN DO WHATEVER YOU CAN TO MAKE THEM MORE PLEASANT. For instance, every Saturday morning, I put on some loud, fun music and do my housework. The music energizes me, and periodically, I stop and dance to a favorite song—so I'm sneaking some exercise in there, too. Grab a friend and share the chores at your house, then go do the cleaning at their house together. Work shared goes much faster!

USE NATURAL PRODUCTS TO CLEAN WITH. They smell better, they're easier on the environment, and best of all, they're cheaper! Most cleaning jobs around the house can be accomplished with nothing more complicated than baking soda and white vinegar—both of which cost just pennies per use. If you want to add a magickal touch, you can put a few drops of any magickal oil into your cleaning solution. For instance, if you want to do some protection magick while you clean the windows, mix vinegar with some water, and add a few drops of your favorite protection oil (see Chapter Five for a few simple recipes), and be sure to visualize as you go.

AT LEAST ONCE A YEAR, OR MORE OFTEN IF NEEDED, DO A THOROUGH "SPIRITUAL SPRING CLEANING" OF YOUR LIVING SPACE. (There are detailed instructions for how to do this in my third book, *The Goddess is in the Details*.) Essentially, you are cleansing the aura or energy of your home, much as you would cleanse your own aura before a ritual. You use many of the same tools, such as sage and salt water—none of which cost much. But the feeling of having a clear and positive home? Priceless.

The Witch's Yard and Garden

Not every Witch is lucky enough to have a yard and a garden (and not every Witch wants one, for that matter). If you do, however, I am sure that you have already found out that they can cost you a *lot* of money if you're not careful.

Obviously, it is nice to have a beautiful yard and a decorative and productive garden, but you don't really have to spend a lot of money to get them. Most of the magickal plants that many Witches use are neither exotic nor pricy, and quite a few herbs have multiple uses: magickal, culinary, and healing, which makes them a triple value.

Here are a few suggestions for ways to make your yard and garden less expensive and more satisfying:

Use seeds. Most flowers, herbs, and vegetables can be grown from seed. This is a much cheaper option than buying plants from a nursery or garden shop. In many cases (although not all, since most hybrid varieties don't breed true from seeds), you can save the seeds a plant produces one year and use them the next. Heirloom seeds are particularly nice for this, and then you have the added benefit of growing a plant with roots in the past (you should excuse the pun). Many folks who use heirloom seeds are enthusiastic about increasing their use and will often provide them for free (or the cost of postage) to anyone who requests them. You can also trade seeds with friends who are gardeners or take turns starting plants from seed by having one of you start all the tomato plants, and one the broccoli, for instance. There are lots of plants (corn, carrots, spinach, lettuce, and radishes, for example) that require nothing more than tossing the seeds into a bit of clear ground and then keeping them relatively free of weeds.

Grow perennials and self-seeding plants. Perennials are plants that come back again year after year and self-seeding plants are those that, while technically not necessarily perennials, tend to reseed themselves without help and show up the next year anyway. Many herbs and flowers fall into these categories. Perennials may cost more to begin with or take more effort to grow from seed, but once they are in your yard or garden, they will come back every year for free. (Be aware that some self-seeding plants are so effective at reproducing themselves that they can take over a yard or garden. Do your research before planting, and make sure that pretty flower isn't considered to be an invasive weed in your area!)

COMPOST. If you have a garden, the easiest and cheapest fertilizer is one you make yourself from scraps and waste you would have otherwise thrown away. Talk about getting something from nothing! Ignore all those fancy, expensive composters you see in the gardening catalogs. They're nice, of course, but all you really need is a spot to pile all the food scraps, yard clippings, and fall leaves. If you want the pile to work faster, you can turn it over occasionally with a spade or a gardening fork. I'm lazy: I pile everything on, ignore it for most of the year, and in the spring, I remove the top layer to uncover the "black gold" underneath. Voila—fertilizer that is wonderful for your plants and easy on your budget.

MAKE THE MOST OF FREE SOURCES. Not only can you use your own scraps and trimmings, but you can also often have other people's waste to add to your pile just by asking. If your neighbors pile their leaves or grass clippings by the curb, ask if you can take them. Many farmers will give you all the manure you want if you are willing to haul it away. Most municipalities create mulch out of the waste they gather, and many of them will let you pick up as much as you can use. This is much cheaper than paying for bags of mulch, and you are recycling, too. If you live in an area with water issues or pay for your water (most folks in the country have wells, which don't cost them anything), collect rain in rain barrels to use in the garden later. Old, clean barrels can be reused by drilling a hole for a spigot at the bottom and placing a screen in the top. There are lots of places online where you can find easy instructions for this. Trade seeds and cuttings with other gardeners and ask your neighbors for cuttings of plants you admire.

GET FREE OR CHEAP TREES. If you want more trees on your property, you can end up spending a lot of money: anywhere from $50 to $200 a tree, usually. But the Arbor Day Foundation gives away trees for the price of a donation (which is tax deductible), and there are often inexpensive trees available through the local Cooperative Extension or other organizations. One of the Blue Moon Circle women moved recently and was able to get fifty small trees (they look like twigs, almost, but grow faster than you can imagine) for around ten dollars.

DON'T USE EXPENSIVE AND HARMFUL PESTICIDES. If you have a garden, you are going to get bugs you don't want. It's just a fact of nature. But don't run to the store and spend lots of money on bug killers. Most of it is highly toxic (and not just to bugs), and there are often simple remedies that work just as well and only cost you pennies. Two of the easiest to use are insecticidal soap and borax. Insecticidal soap is simple to make—just mix 3% dish soap with water (you may need to try a few different brands to find one that works well or increase the percentage of soap) and spray on your plants. It is completely non-toxic and either keeps off or kills many garden pests. Borax is a common laundry additive that is also non-toxic to humans and pets, but amazingly effective at keeping away ants and other bugs. It can be used by itself, but when I have ant infestations, I mix it with powdered sugar (also cheap) and sprinkle it outside around my foundation and inside near the site of the infestation. The ants eat the sugar/borax mix and then disappear. If necessary, you can clean up the remainder in a week or so, but I find that it mostly vanishes with the ants.

Don't forget the magickal plants. One of the best things about being a Witch with a garden or yard is the ability to grow your own plants for magickal use. Many of the herbs we use for cooking also have their magickal uses; some Witches even keep a separate magickal garden and grow the plants within it with the intention of using them for spells and rituals. This gives you the opportunity to infuse your herbs with magickal intent from the moment you place their seeds in the ground, which can give them quite a lot of oomph, magickally speaking. And you aren't limited to herbs, either—many common flowers, shrubs, and trees have their magickal uses, too, as well as being decorative in your yard. If you don't know where to start, try one of the great books on magickal plants and gardening listed on page 24.

Whether you are a Country Witch with a large garden or a City Witch with a tiny apartment, your home is an important part of both your mundane and your spiritual life. Without spending much money, you can create an oasis of calm and beauty that will reflect your spirit and your Pagan path. And with the money you have left over, you can even buy a few extra candles for those times when you *want* the lights to be off.

CHAPTER 4

USE THIS, NOT THAT:
INEXPENSIVE SUBSTITUTES FOR
EXPENSIVE ITEMS

Odds are you are going to end up spending at least *some* money on your practice of the Craft. How much will depend on your priorities, your budget, and your ability to make some of what you need for yourself, among other factors.

Priorities play a big part in choosing which items you spend your hard-earned cash on. As I mentioned before, books are one of my biggest expenditures. This is in part because I consider learning about Wicca and the subjects associated with Witchcraft to be one of the most important components of following my path. It is also because, although there is a lot of information available for free online, I like to have my resources on hand (and I use other authors' books quite often as research for my own).

So, I decided long ago that I would rather spend my money on books than almost anything else. But I also have some other items—like drums, crystals, and various candles—that I either couldn't make for myself or thought weren't worth the time and energy it would take to do so. (For instance, I used to make my own candles. Lots of fun and I still have the supplies, but I simply don't have the free time anymore. So, I usually buy pre-made candles and make them more special by anointing them with oil or carving them with symbols of my magickal working.)

On the other hand, many of the Pagan supplies that other folks pay for, I've either made for myself (like my cloak, or the herbs I've grown in my garden) or found inexpensive substitutes for.

Just because a book says, "Take a pink candle and a cup of rose petals," for instance, doesn't mean that those are the only possible items to use for that particular spell. If you don't want to spend the money on rose petals, for example, you could use a less expensive flower, a single rose, or even a picture of a rose. If you are given flowers (or buy them for yourself), you can get in the habit of saving the petals from any that have magickal uses and drying them for later use.

Obviously, there are certain supplies that are particularly useful and often aren't terribly expensive—most candles and herbs are relatively cheap if you know the right places to get them. And sometimes it is faster and easier to use something expensive, even if it costs more than making it yourself or finding an alternative. If time is more valuable than money, sometimes it is better to just buy the tricky stuff. Not to mention that not everyone is crafty or has the space to grow their own magickal plants.

However, there are a great many components of magickal work that can be found in less expensive forms or replaced by something else altogether. Here are some suggestions that might save you a buck or two. Or even twenty.

THE CIRCLE. Some folks buy flat pavers or large river stones for the outline of their outdoor circles, and these are undoubtedly impressive. For a less ornate permanent circle, use stones you find on your own property (if you have them, and if you don't mind hauling them), or a bag of decorative white stones for the garden (about five dollars a bag—but be aware that unless you clear away the grass, they will eventually disappear). Or dig a couple of inches into the earth and let the bare place be your circle. For a temporary circle outside, use flowers laid in a circular pattern (it works especially well if you have flowers with long stems, which luckily, many wildflowers do), shells (this is especially good if you happen to live by the water and shells are abundant and free) or salt. For an inside circle, you can get a large piece of canvas or some other inexpensive cloth and paint a circle on it, maybe with a pentacle in the middle and symbols for the four quarters at the appropriate places and roll it up out of the way when it's not in use. Flowers will work inside too, or you can use salt or chalk to draw the circle on the floor if you don't mind cleaning up the mess afterward.

FANCY FIREPIT. There is nothing witchier than an outside circle with a blazing bonfire in the middle (especially on Samhain night). And there are some amazing cast iron firepits available these days with stars and moons on the sides, and others that are made out of burnished copper. But if you're not made out of money, you can always do the cheapest alternative: dig a hole in the ground. The least expensive way to have a bonfire is to simply dig a firepit in the ground, line the rim with rocks if you want to, and fill it with logs and branches from your own property. However, if you can't do that, try using a large metal cauldron (make sure it is made out of something like iron that can stand the heat)—you can sometimes find used ones that are much cheaper than new ones. Another alternative, especially if you can't have an actual bonfire due to location, fire regulations, or being stuck inside, is to fill a cauldron or bowl with sand (or salt) and then stick candles into the sand (a box of white "emergency" candles is usually less than three dollars, and they work just fine). Or you can use a bunch of tea lights, which are even cheaper. They make a pretty light, and the flickering of the candles will mimic some of the feeling of a bonfire.

Elaborate Candleholders. Candleholders designed especially for Pagans come in an amazing variety of styles: everything from cast iron medieval reproductions to ceramic dragons breathing fire. Most of them are pretty cool, but they all cost a pretty penny, too. If you want candleholders for outdoor rituals, try looking at a local hardware or garden shop; many of them have relatively inexpensive cast iron candleholders and oil torches that are designed to be stuck in the ground. I once found ones that even came with your choice of red, green, yellow, or blue citronella candles already in them; I got one of each and had instant quarter candles for the outside circle. Cost? Five dollars apiece, and the candles lasted for two years! You can also build your own simple outdoor candleholder out of copper pipe (use a piece of end-pipe to hold the candle), or PVC (which you can then paint with the quarter colors or any designs you like). Other options include using old jars (which you can fill with sand to help the candles stand up), and large citronella sticks (like huge incense, but made out of citronella to get rid of mosquitoes, these can also be found in varied colors), metal or pottery plates or bowls (make sure these are fire safe, and they will work best with either tea lights, votives, or large pillar candles). If you want something fancier without spending a lot of money, try using floating candles in pretty glass or pottery goblets.

Spell Candles. I love looking at the spell candles in Pagan stores and catalogs; candles for love and prosperity, candles with herbs in them or anointed with magickal oils, candles carved with runes for protection or healing. You can find specially designed candles for every need and in every color. But you'll pay a lot extra for the fact that somebody else has put the magick into the candle for you. Instead, try buying inexpensive candles (make sure they are unscented if you want to put your own magickal touches on them) at the dollar store or after the holiday season when they may be on clearance sales (you can pick up green and red ones after Christmas, for instance). Go to yard sales and find barely-used candles; if you don't like the idea of using pre-used candles for ritual work, you can always melt them down and make them new again. And there are a few simple candle ideas in the craft section of Chapter Five. Or just use the plain votives sold in most Pagan stores for between a dollar or two. Sometimes if you buy them in bulk, they're cheaper. If you aren't particularly crafty but still want to dress up a plain candle, you can tie a ribbon around it in the color appropriate for the spell you are doing. You can even write the spell on the ribbon itself if the spell is short enough or the ribbon wide enough. Just make sure that the candle doesn't burn down far enough to set the ribbon on fire!

QUARTER CANDLES. Quarter candles are a little different from spell candles. Many Witches light a candle for each quarter: yellow for East, red for South, green for North, and blue for West. But do you have to do it this way? Of course not. For one thing, if all you have are white candles, that's fine. You can tie colored string or yarn in the quarter colors at the base of the candles, place them in appropriately colored candle holders, or on colored plates. Or you can do without candles altogether. (Under some circumstances, like a college dorm room or most hotels, for example, you aren't allowed to have candles or open flames. These are great alternatives for those times as well.) Try using symbols of Earth, Air, Fire, and Water: a rock, a feather, an unlit candle or a picture of a flame, and a seashell or a cup of water. Or you can use four flowers in the quarter colors, or four gemstones (try lapis, aventurine, yellow jade, and red jasper—if you get them in the form of tumbled stones, they shouldn't cost more than a dollar each, maybe less). Bryanna B., one of the women in my first group, uses four rocks with different qualities: mica or pumice for Air, lava or obsidian for Fire, sandstone or limestone for Earth, and a beach or river rock for Water. And a bunch of rocks is great if you are still in the broom closet—nothing Witchy going on here, no sir.

GARB. For most of us, dressing as a Witch isn't restricted to Halloween. (If you want to be literal, no matter what we're wearing, we're dressed as Witches. So those footsie pajamas are really Witch clothes, too.) Generally referred to as "garb," these are the special clothes we wear only for rituals or Pagan gatherings. For some folks, this means a velvet cloak, a long flowing dress or drawstring pants, or a silk robe embroidered with mystical symbols. Others wear elaborate outfits suitable for Renaissance Faires, or robes of plain white silk or cotton. Store-bought (or catalog-bought) garb can run into hundreds of dollars; maybe more if you actually fall in love with something fancy when you're at the Faire. But garb doesn't have to cost you the shirt off your back. The main point is to have something that is different from your everyday clothes; preferably something a little dressier, made out of natural fibers, that you can move comfortably in. (That lets out anything with boning in the bodice, as far as I'm concerned!) Here are a few options:

First, if you have any sewing ability, you can make your own garb. I made my own cloak for about a quarter of the cost of what it would have cost me to buy one, and it wasn't very difficult. When you make it yourself, you know it will be the right size, the color and shape you want, and a material you can take care of easily. Try looking for patterns at the local Walmart (I admit it—I can't stand this store—but sometimes they really do have the best bargains); they are on sale there every day. Or for something like a cloak, see if you can share the pattern with someone else since one size pretty much fits all. In the case of something simple, like a cloak or a robe, you can sometimes do without a pattern altogether and just cut out the material based on an already-existing garment. Don't feel like you have to pay top dollar and get the fanciest material, either. Velvet cloaks are wonderful, but you can make a lovely ritual cloak out of velveteen or moleskin, both of which are much less expensive. (And moleskin, which my cloak is made out of, has the added benefit of being slightly water-repellent, for when the rain starts coming down in the middle of your ritual.) Many basic magickal garments are loose and flowy, making them fairly simple to sew.

If you aren't a seamstress or have no time or inclination to make your own garb, you can look for clothing items that already have the appearance of garb: old Halloween costumes, for instance (find an Elvira one, and you're all set!), or the aforementioned Renaissance Faire outfits. Try looking on eBay or at yard sales for items that people have outgrown or no longer use.

Take everyday clothing that has a witchy look to it and dedicate it as ritual garb. For example, a lacy black shirt and a flowing black skirt can look very magickal when paired together. I have a lot of hippy/peasant-type clothes that make great garb. For others, a black or white pirate shirt and a pair of black pants work well.

Take everyday clothes and add a witchy touch. Try putting an iron-on pentacle or Green Man on a plain tee-shirt or adding ribbons to a simple skirt. (Azure Green has a large supply of Pagan-themed patches, for instance, or you can buy special computer supplies and print out iron-on designs at home.) Lace can dress up anything, and lighter-colored garments can be tie-dyed or decorated with fabric paints. Your imagination is the only limit.

JEWELRY. Pagans love their jewelry. Almost every Witch has at least one pentacle necklace (I have about a dozen, but I'm a jewelry maker, so that's my excuse.) Many of us also have special rings, bracelets, and earrings as well. One of the great aspects of jewelry is that it takes the plainest outfit and turns it into witchy garb. Also, you can tuck your necklace under your shirt so no one is the wiser or wear it proudly so all your Pagan brothers and sisters know who you are. But witchy jewelry can be as expensive as magickal garb—or even more so if you have a taste for gemstone and silver (and what Witch doesn't?). There are a few ways to make yourself decorative without making your bank statement downright ugly.

Keep it simple. A basic silver pentacle on a chain doesn't have to cost a lot of money, especially if it is small (and the chain itself doesn't have to be silver, either).

Mix up your metals. Try getting a pentacle in copper or pewter, either of which should be much cheaper than silver.

Adopt a popular symbol. If you don't want to wear a pentacle, it is pretty easy to find jewelry that features other Pagan symbols, such as moons, stars, Celtic crosses, and spirals. If you don't have to get your jewelry from a specialty store (Pagan or New Age), you are likelier to find it at a price you can afford.

Make it yourself. Jewelry making is a fairly easy craft to master, and the supplies are readily available. If you want to wear a gemstone necklace or bracelet but don't want to pay top dollar, you can try making one yourself. (If you are in a coven, try making it a group project, so you can share the costs of getting the tools and supplies you need.)

Think outside the box. Instead of spending a hundred dollars on a sterling silver headpiece with a crescent moon on it, try buying a dollar's worth of silver ribbon and either draw a symbol on the front or dangle a small charm from the middle.

Athames and Swords. Both these tools have essentially the same purpose, although they are used slightly differently. The athame is a ritual knife that is used for directing energy and occasionally mixing or stirring (such as when you combine salt and water in a bowl). A ritual sword is also used to direct energy. Both may be utilized in casting the circle, and the athame is often also used to call the quarters. But while these are great tools to have, you don't really need them. Swords are traditionally used for Ceremonial Magick and some of the more traditional coven traditions, like Alexandrian. If you are a solitary or practicing in a more eclectic coven, it is unlikely you will need a sword at all. An athame is a more commonly used tool and can vary from the simple and relatively inexpensive to the ornate and insanely pricy. A handcrafted athame can cost hundreds of dollars, while a short, wooden-handled one can be as little as six. But if you don't want to spend any money at all, you have an equivalent tool as close as the end of your hand. Since the main purpose of the athame is directing energy, you can just use your finger to point instead. Alternately, an attractive stick can serve the same purpose. Look for one that feels right to you (you'll know it when you find it), and if you want, decorate it with magickal symbols, carve it, or add a ribbon or two.

Magick Wand. Sadly, most of us don't have a Harry Potter wand that really does magick. This is another tool that is used to point and direct energy. And like the athame, you can find some beautifully made (and very pricy) handcrafted wands created out of anything from wood to copper to silver, many of them with gemstones and crystals attached. Even a simple wood wand can run you a lot of money; the really fancy ones can be hundreds or even thousands. But you can easily make your own wand from a piece of wood—the simplest ones don't require anything more than finding a pretty piece of wood the right size and shape and consecrating it for magickal work. If you want something more ornate, you can glue or bind gemstones, feathers, shells, or ribbons to it and add runic carvings or magickal symbols. But all you really need is a bit of branch that has fallen to the ground, and you're good to go. If you want a smooth wand, find a nice stick, strip the bark off, sand it with three grades of sandpaper (starting with rough and ending with fine), then oil it if desired. Or, if you live by the beach, you can look for a special piece of driftwood that the power of water has already turned into the perfect wand.

CAULDRONS. A cauldron is usually a deep cast iron bowl that stands on three legs. Traditionally used for mixing magickal brews and other spell components, they can also be utilized for ritual fires, as scrying bowls (when filled with water), or for burning granular incense. Some cauldrons are food-safe, but many are not and should not be used for anything that will actually be consumed. Cauldrons come in a variety of sizes, from tiny (which are usually used as altar pieces) to gigantic (which can take three people to set into place for ritual). I found my medium-sized cauldron at a street-wide garage sale for thirty dollars a number of years ago. You can try looking for them on places like eBay, but since they tend to be heavy, any money you save on the item itself is likely to be spent on shipping. Instead, try looking in flea markets or other places that specialize in used items. Or you can substitute an inexpensive cast iron hibachi, the kind that is often sold for about ten dollars during barbeque season. Alternately, any fire-safe bowl will do.

CHALICE. Most Witches use a chalice to hold the wine or juice for "Cakes and Ale" or for the libation they pour to the gods during a ritual. A chalice is essentially a goblet of some kind, and they can vary from simple pottery to ornate silver decorated with goddesses, gemstones, dragons, or pentacles. I have seen some amazing (and pricy) handmade chalices in my travels. I'd love to own one someday, I admit. But for the moment, I am perfectly happy with the pottery chalice I bought for ten dollars from a local artisan. My coven, Blue Moon Circle, is lucky enough to have a potter as a member, and she made us a group goblet that we all decorated together before she gave it the final firing. If you can't find an inexpensive ceramic goblet that suits your needs, you can always use a wine glass that you set aside for ritual purposes. I've seen perfectly nice ones in the dollar store, in fact. If you want to dress up a simple glass goblet, you can buy a few inexpensive markers that are made to be permanent when used on glass. Or look in flea markets, garage sales, or even antique stores for interesting goblets. You can probably get a good deal if there is only one left out of what was originally a set. You can also use a small bowl if you choose.

GOD AND GODDESS STATUES. It is nice to have something to represent the God and Goddess (or whichever deity or deities you follow) on your altar. But these don't need to be expensive works of art. Try substituting a silver candle for the Goddess and a gold candle for the God. Or anything that might represent them, such as a piece of horn or antler for the God, and anything open (a shell or a cup, for instance) to symbolize the womb of the Goddess. Other alternatives are a picture or plaque of the Tree of Life or anything that can be used to stand for the essence of female and male. If you worship a particular god or goddess, you can also use something that symbolizes that deity in particular—a cat for Bast, for instance, or a small cauldron for Brigid.

Tarot Cards, Rune Stones, Crystal Balls. There are various tools that are used by Witches for divination; which one (if any) that you chose is usually determined by what works best for you. I have one deck of tarot cards that I've been using for years (I read professionally), and a number of runes sets, some of which I've made myself. Tarot decks in particular are available in an astonishing array of beautiful and tempting forms, and it is easy to spend a lot of money on them just because they're so darned cool looking. But if you want to practice divination on a shoestring, there are a number of alternatives to expensive premade tools. The next chapter has instructions for simple and easy rune stones, for instance. Or you can make your own tarot cards by printing out the images on sturdy paper and cutting them into card shapes. You can learn to do divination with regular playing cards, too. There are also instructions for making your own tarot cards and a handmade scrying mirror in the next chapter as well. The cheapest and easiest methods for scrying involve nothing more than a dark bowl filled with water—just clear your mind, ask a question, and look.

Book of Shadows. Most Witches have at least one Book of Shadows. In it, they write down everything from spells and rituals to herbal lore, dreams, and goals for the future. There are many lovely Books of Shadows that are made for just this purpose; some of them even have leather or carved wood covers, gemstones glued on, or other special ornamentation that lifts them from the mundane to the sublime. But you don't need to spend a lot of money to get a special book in which to keep your magickal work. You can use any notebook, journal, or blank book, some of which are quite nice (and while they won't come with pentacles or goddesses on the front, you might well be able to find one with faeries, cats, dragons, or nature scenes). I have a few Books of Shadows, including one that I bought and one that I made from a three-ring binder (mostly used for holding information I've printed out or copied from somewhere, like Sabbat correspondences, healing techniques, and other reference information I'll only refer to from time to time) and decorated with magickal symbols. In the chapter on crafts, I'll show you how to take an inexpensive pre-made blank book and create a sacred Book of Shadows of your own.

One final note on buying magickal tools and allocating money for your practice of the Craft—sometimes spending money is a good thing. Obviously, you want to spend your money wisely: buy only those things that you will treasure and/or use often, or that you can't make for yourself, find a decent substitute for, or do without. But also keep in mind that it is important to support and contribute to the magickal community. As I mentioned in the chapter on knowledge, if none of us ever bought a new book at full price, they'd stop publishing Pagan books—and that would be tragic.

In the same way, if we don't at least occasionally purchase items from Pagan shops, online Witchcraft stores, and individual Pagan craftspeople, all these people and places will go out of business—and then we'd have no place to get the magickal tools we need when we finally do decide to buy something special.

All we can do is try to balance our need to be frugal with our desire to support the greater Pagan community and choose wisely when we spend our hard-earned cash.

Here are a few good sources for reasonably priced magickal tools and supplies. Some of these shops exist only online and some have physical locations.

- *13moons.com*
- *AzureGreen.com* (Azure Green 16 Bell Rd PO Box 48 Middlefield, MA 01243)
- *Isisbooks.com*
- *Sacredmists.com*
- *Theblessedbee.com*

CHAPTER 5

THE CRAFTY WITCH:
THIRTY-FIVE SIMPLE AND THRIFTY
CRAFT PROJECTS FOR MAGICKAL
PURPOSES

Witchcraft is often referred to as "the Craft," and much of the practice of Witchcraft involves creativity, imagination, and making something out of nothing. Little wonder, then, that so many Witches are also attracted to crafting of other types as well.

Crafting the elements of your spellwork gives you the chance to put your energy and intention into the working at a much deeper level. For this reason alone, it is worth trying your hand at a magickal craft or two. But many tools and magickal ingredients are also much cheaper if you make them yourself, and creating such things gives you the freedom to express yourself and lend a personal touch to your magickal toolbox.

Obviously, you are unlikely to do every single craft idea in this chapter (although more power to you if you can). I suggest you look at the various possibilities and start with the ones that appeal to you most. The crafts are grouped by medium: clay, wax, string & yarn, fabric, herbs & plants, wood, paper, glass, and stone. But this doesn't mean that there won't be some overlap; for instance, herbs in one form or another are used in many of the projects.

I have also given each project a symbol to denote the ease or difficulty of each task. None of them are very complicated, but the simplest has one star, and the most complicated has three. If you're not a particularly "crafty" person, you might want to start with the one-star projects first, just to get your feet wet.

Many of these projects lend themselves well to group work, so if you happen to be in a coven or have a bunch of witchy friends, you may want to work on the crafts together. If you do so, you may want to use the activity as a time to discuss your goals and what you each hope to get out of the magickal endeavor. Some items, like the Yule wreath, can be collaborated on together, to make one large project instead of a number of small, individual ones. In fact, most of these craft projects originated from the practice that Blue Moon Circle has done together over the years.

Before you get started, make sure you have all the necessary supplies and ingredients for the craft project you have chosen to do. Almost all the items listed in this chapter should be readily available at local stores—grocery stores, super centers, health food stores, Pagan, or New Age stores. If you are lucky enough to have a craft shop where you live, that will certainly help, but it shouldn't be necessary. In very few cases, you might have to order supplies online if you live in a small town like I do, where there are fewer shopping options.

Some items might be easiest to find at specialty stores, such as sewing or hardware stores, but you will be surprised by how many of the supplies you already have lying around the house. Most of us have the basics, like needle and thread, bits of cloth, pieces of wood, and old bottles. The rest of the ingredients shouldn't cost you more than ten dollars—and often, they'll be available for considerably less. I'll also suggest places to look for any of the more unusual supplies. Don't forget that when you do a project with your friends, you can all chip in on the ingredients, which can make it much cheaper.

Remember that any magickal project can be made even more powerful by consecrating and blessing the item after you make it, if you so choose. In some cases, this step is built right into the process, but even if it isn't, you can always take a few moments after you're finished with your new creation and dedicate it for magickal work.

CLAY

God and Goddess Figures *

Supplies:
- Clay (one container of clay should be enough to make all three of these projects).
- Seeds
- Toothpicks or other pointed tools.
- Bowl of water and paper towels (for cleaning hands).
- Something to protect whatever surface you're working on.

Notes:
The easiest kind of clay to use for this project is the type that can be dried by leaving it out in the air (self-hardening). That way you don't need anything fancy like a kiln. It can be found in most craft or art supply stores, or the craft sections of department stores. Oven-bake polymer clay can also be used. It doesn't really matter what kind of seeds you use, although smaller ones may be easier to work

with (large smooth seeds like pumpkin seeds, for instance, may not stick well in the clay). When Blue Moon Circle did this project, we used calendula seeds—in part, because they are symbolic of healing, and in part, because I had grown them in my garden, so they were free! You may want to use seeds from a plant that has a magickal use that ties in with your goals if you have any particular ones.

Magical Uses:

This project was originally created as part of a "Spring Re-birthing" ritual (see Chapter Seven in my first book, *Circle, Coven & Grove: A Year of Magickal Practice* for that ritual and the spell that went with it). The intent was to create a Goddess image (or God image) that was the essence of your perfect self—so each of us envisioned ourselves as our own Goddess (or God). As you might imagine, each coven member's Goddess statue was completely different from the others. (One woman even made herself in an egg shape to denote the potential she felt was waiting inside her.) You can also use this project to create God and Goddess statues for your altar or a figure for healing magick.

Directions:

- Take enough clay to fit in your two palms and roll it back and forth until it is soft and mallea-ble. If necessary, add a little water to make the self-hardening clay more workable.
- Using your fingers and any tools you find helpful, shape the clay into a woman (Goddess figure). If you are creating a Goddess in your own image, you may want to give it some of your own features or improve on anything you might consider to be a flaw or a goal for change. (You can make a God figure instead, of course—or you may want to do both if you want a set for your altar.)

- When you have the statue the way you want it, press seeds into it as decoration or to symbolize the magickal work you want to do with the figure. For instance, if you are using the statue for healing work, use seeds from a plant associated with healing (such as calendula, echinacea, or lemon balm), and place them on the areas where you need healing the most.
- Remember to focus on your magickal goals as you are working the clay so they become a part of the finished statue.

AFTERWARD:
- Once the statue is dry, you can place it on your altar. If you created the figure for a particular magickal task, such as healing or rebirth, you may eventually want to bury it outside where the seeds can sprout and carry your intent out into the world.

Rune Stones ✶ ✶

SUPPLIES:
- Self-hardening clay.
- Toothpick or pointed tool for carving.
- Book or picture of runes stones or another premade set you can copy from if you don't have all the runes memorized.
- A bowl of water and some paper towels (to clean your hands as needed).
- Something to protect the surface you are working on.
- Optional: drawstring bag of cotton or velvet to put your runes in when they're done.

Notes:

This is perhaps a little more difficult to do than the first project, but still easy enough if you go slowly and carefully. Most rune symbols are fairly simple to draw, even if that's not your best skill (it's not mine, I assure you). And the great thing about clay is if you mess it up, you can just smoosh it and start all over!

Magickal Uses:

Rune stones are used for telling fortunes, in much the same way as tarot cards are. However, many people find them easier to use, since there is a little less interpretation needed on the part of the reader. Also, they're fun to use. The simplest way to do a rune reading is to just put all the stones in a bag, or lay them upside down on the table, then ask your question and pull one or more runes to get the answer. The benefit to making your own set, besides saving money by not buying expensive pre-made runes, is that you put much of your own energy into making them. This can only help you later on when you use them to get answers for yourself or for others.

Directions:

- You will be making 24 or 25 rune stones, each the same size and shape (they can be as small or large as you like but are usually around an inch square). Some people use a blank rune (the 25th stone) and others don't.
- It is probably easiest to form all the rune stones first, and then decorate them after you've done so. But there's no reason that you can't do them one at a time if you prefer.
- Work the clay until it is malleable, adding a bit of water if necessary. You can roll the clay out

and cut the individual rune stones or simply form them with your fingers (that's what I did).

- Once you have the stones made, carve each one with a different rune symbol. If you want to get a bit fancier, you can decorate the backs by carving a symbol (such as a crescent moon, a pentacle, or your initials) or use a rubber stamp or some other object to stamp an identical picture onto each one. (If you are using a stamp, you may find it works best to do that side first, and then carve the rune symbol—otherwise, you risk mashing your design as you stamp the other side.)

- If you want to get really fancy (and spend a bit more money), you can use different colors of polymer clay.

AFTERWARD:

- Once the clay has dried, you can store your rune stones in a drawstring bag, an old wooden box, or any handy container with a magickal flare. If you plan to use them at all seriously, I highly recommend consecrating and blessing them first.

Pentacle Plaque ✶ ✶

SUPPLIES:
- Self-hardening clay.
- Toothpicks or pointed tools for drawing with.
- Bowl of water and paper towels (for cleaning your hands as needed)
- Something to protect the surface you are working on.
- Optional: rolling pin.

NOTES:

This project can be as simple or as complicated as you choose to make it. Folks with serious artistic talent (of which I am not one, alas) can make an ornate and detailed plaque. Other people may choose to keep it simple and limit themselves to carving out a pentacle in the center with a few other symbols around the edges. If you want to hang the plaque when you are done (as opposed to laying it down on a flat surface or leaning it again the wall behind your altar, for instance), you will want to put a hole in the back that will fit over a nail after the piece has dried.

MAGICKAL USES:

A pentacle plaque is essentially decorative; a symbol of your path as a Pagan. You can, however, make a plaque to represent a particular magickal working (if you are doing magickal work to bring love into your life, for instance, you can carve hearts into it, or male and/or female symbols), then hang it over your altar to remind you to focus on your goal. If you are using the plaque for spellwork, it is best to make the plaque either right beforehand or as a part of the ritual.

DIRECTIONS:

- Work the clay until it is soft and malleable, adding a bit of water if necessary.
- You may want to roll out the clay to make it more uniform in shape. Cut or form the clay into whatever shape you want: your plaque can be round, oval, square, or rectangular.
- If you want to make the edges more decorative, you can press something textured into them or give them scallops or ridges.
- Using a pointed object or a toothpick, carefully draw a pentacle shape lightly in the middle of your plaque. Once you have it looking the way you want it, then go ahead and carve it a bit deeper. Add other symbols around the sides of the pentacle as desired: symbols for the four quarters, for instance, or the phases of the moon.
- If you are using the plaque for a particular magickal task, you will want to use symbols that are appropriate for that task (see note above). Make sure that your finished project feels whole and balanced to you.

AFTERWARD:

- After the clay dries, hang the plaque above your altar or place it on the altar or any surface where you will look at it often.

WAX

Crafting Candles (Beeswax and Paraffin) ✶ ✶ ✶

SUPPLIES:

- Depending on which kind of candles you are making; you will need either paraffin wax or beeswax.
- You can also make candles by melting down the ends of previously used candles if you don't want to spend the money on new supplies.
- Bits of old crayons or used candles can be used instead of dye (although the dye works a little better).
- The only thing you absolutely have to buy new is candle wicking (the thickness will depend on the width of your candle, check the instructions on the wick package).
- A stick of some kind to hold the wick above the mold (a chopstick or a pencil works fine).
- Something to use as a mold. Sturdy glass jars such as pint-sized canning jars work well. You can also use muffin tins, empty frozen juice containers, and just about anything else that can stand up to hot wax instead of buying fancy candle molds (you can also use a decorative tin as long as you are sure it doesn't leak. Check it with water first).
- Optional: You can also add scent if you want to. I like to use a magickal oil to give the candle an extra magickal boost. A double boiler can be used for melting wax (don't use one you will want to cook in again—try looking at a second-hand store for a used one) or you can float a tin can in a pot of water.

NOTES:

There are a wide array of candle-making supplies available, all of them fun, and some of them not that expensive. Paraffin can be found in small amounts in the canning section of the grocery store or at craft stores. Beeswax comes in a number of forms; the simplest to use is a sheet that you simply soften slightly and roll up, but it also comes as little pebbles which you melt down. Beeswax tends to be more expensive than paraffin, but if you are only making one or two candles, it shouldn't set you back too much. Be aware that beeswax is a natural substance and paraffin comes from petroleum. Beeswax will need to be purchased at a craft shop or online. Paraffin will be easier to find, as will old candles, which often turn up at yard sales if you don't happen to have any around. BE VERY CAREFUL WHEN MELTING THE WAX. Candle wax has to be melted slowly and carefully or it can catch on fire. Water will not put out a wax fire, so it is a good idea to have a container of salt around to smother it and a fire extinguisher just in case. Use a stove temperature that is just high enough to keep the water at a simmer and be patient.

MAGICKAL USES:

Candles can be used for all kinds of magick. Try making one that uses the color that coordinates with whatever magick you want to use it for. And remember to concentrate on your intention as you stir the wax so that each movement adds to the magickal power of your candle.

DIRECTIONS:
- If you are using a sheet of beeswax, all you have to do is warm it slightly so it is malleable and roll the sheet up with a wick inside, leaving a bit of the wick sticking out the top. This is the easiest way to make your own candles (but not the cheapest).

- Note that the following instructions are the same whether you are using new wax, beeswax pellets, re-using old wax, or any combination of the three.
- Arrange the container you will be using with the wick centered above (wrapping the wick around a pencil and propping the pencil on top of the container usually works well).
- In a double boiler or a can inside a pot, place your wax, chopped up into smallish pieces. (The smaller the pieces, the faster they melt.)
- Slowly melt the wax, stirring periodically to keep the heat spread throughout. When the wax is completely melted, you can add any color or magickal oils you are using.
- Turn the heat off and stir until the color is melted and the oil is dispersed (you don't need to use very much oil, 5-10 drops will do).
- Working over a heat-safe surface (such as a counter with wax paper spread over it—DO NOT do this over the stove, as any wax you spill will be a royal pain to clean up), pour the wax into the container, taking care not to soak the very top of the wick.
- Fill the container as high as you want without going over the edges. If you are using a largish mold, the wax will form a depression in the middle as it cools, and you may have to re-melt the remaining wax and add a little more. The time the wax takes to set will depend on the diameter of the candle.

AFTERWARD:
- Burn your candle as part of a ritual or spell, or simply use it on its own. Never leave a candle burning without supervision.

Creating a Healing Candle ✴

Supplies:
- A pillar candle (this can be a candle you made yourself or one you purchased).
- Various healing herbs (you can use whichever ones appeal to you; some of my favorites are lemon balm, lavender, rosemary, and calendula but there are many, many, many to choose from) either fresh or dried.
- Optional: white glue, any magickal healing oil (see instructions for making these later in the chapter), waxed paper.

Notes:
There are a few different ways to do this, and some are simpler than others. You can experiment to see which one works best for you.

Magickal Uses:
Healing (although you can also use this same project to make other magickal candles, just substitute the appropriate herbs for that work).

Directions:
- The simplest way to do this project is to spread your herbs out on a safe surface (waxed paper works well), spread a thin layer of white glue onto the sides of the candle, and roll the candle in the herbs.
- If you don't like the idea of using glue, you can either soften the candle wax slightly by heating it over a warm flame or burner (only until it softens, you don't want to actually melt the candle) or melt a little bit of additional wax that

you spread on the candle instead of the glue. Then roll the candle in the herbs as before.

- If you want to add a little oomph to your magickal work, try carving symbols for healing (including the name or initials of whoever the candle is for) into the candle before applying the herbs. Or you can apply the melted wax or glue in a pattern (such as a pentacle or a healing rune) and then add the herbs.
- You can also add a few drops of healing magickal oil to your herbs or anoint the candle with it once you are finished.

AFTERWARD:

- Once the wax or glue has dried, burn the candle as usual. Keep a careful eye on it to make sure that the herbs don't smoke or burn as the candle is used. (Hint: a wide pillar candle often doesn't burn all the way to the outside, so it might be good to use one of that type for this particular project.)
- If you want, you can say this spell (from my book, *The Goddess is in the Details*) when you light your candle:

I call upon the gods above
In perfect trust, in perfect love
I ask for health and energy
Balanced and in synergy
Healthy body, mind, and soul
A perfect, balanced, healthy whole
I pledge that I will do my part
For healthy body, healthy heart
Every day, let health increase
Until all signs of illness cease

Inscribing and Anointing Candles for Prosperity ✶

SUPPLIES:
- Candle (green is good for prosperity work, but white or gold are fine, too).
- Toothpick or another pointed object for carving.
- Essential oil or magickal oil (see instructions for making magickal oils later in this chapter).
- Something to protect the surface you are working on.

NOTES:

When you anoint candles, you are actually combining candle magick with herbal magick.

DIRECTIONS:
- Candles can be inscribed with any symbols for prosperity you prefer. I often use various runes that work well for prosperity, such as Gifu (gifts), Ing (success), Jera (rewards), Sigel (power and success), and Fehu (material gain, money). You can also inscribe your initials or name, dollar signs, or anything else that seems appropriate.
- Use a toothpick or another pointed object (such as the tip of your athame) and carve the symbols into the surface of the candle.
- Use a drop or two of oil to anoint the candle, starting at the bottom and working your way up. Good oils for prosperity include basil, cinnamon, clove, ginger, patchouli, sandalwood, and spearmint. (Remember, if you are combining a few different ones, you want to use oils that go well together.)
- Remember to focus on your goal as you work.

AFTERWARD:
- Burn your candle on a Thursday, a Full Moon, or whenever you need that boost of prosperity the most.
- If you don't have a prosperity spell you prefer, feel free to use mine (first published in *Circle, Coven & Grove: A Year of Magickal Practice*)

God and Goddess
Hear my plea
Rain prosperity
Down on me
Bring in monies
Large and small
To pay my bills
One and all

Magickal Wax Tablets ✶ ✶

SUPPLIES:
- Block of paraffin wax.
- A pointed object for carving.
- Optional: flat piece of wood, double boiler.

NOTES:
Wax tablets are an ancient writing tool. Wax would be melted over a slab of wood, the writing would be gouged into the wax, and when it was no longer needed, the wax would be melted down and reused. You can do the same thing or carve symbols into your wax and leave it permanently.

MAGICKAL USES:
Like the pentacle plaque described earlier in the chapter, these wax tablets can be used purely for decoration. But they can also be used to create a concrete manifestation of your magickal work. For instance, if you are doing a

spell for prosperity, you can carve the symbols mentioned in the section above, then place the tablet on your altar for a month or so before melting the wax down to use again.

DIRECTIONS:
- There are two ways to do this particular project. The first and simplest uses only wax. In this case, you can either slice (slowly and carefully) though the piece of wax with a heated knife (you will probably have to heat and reheat the knife, and it must be sharp, so be careful not to cut yourself) or melt the wax and pour it into a square or rectangular container. A small disposable aluminum pan, for instance.
- Or, if you want to be more authentic, you can get a square or rectangular piece of wood (something about the size of a paperback book will do).
- Melt some wax and pour it carefully onto the surface of the wood so you have a uniform coating of half an inch to an inch thick.
- No matter which form you use, wait until the wax is solid again, then use a pointed tool to draw or carve your symbols into the wax. If you find the wax difficult to carve, you can try heating the end of your tool a bit.
- Carve decorative symbols, or ones that go with your magickal working, then place the tablet on your altar or someplace where you will see it on a regular basis.

AFTERWARD:
- If you are using the wax tablet for spellwork, once you have achieved your aim (or feel that the energy you put into the working has been used up), you can scrape it off, re-melt the wax, and use it for another spell.

STRING & YARN

Goddess's Eye Charm ✳

SUPPLIES:
- Wooden popsicle sticks (available in most craft sections, or if you really want to be thrifty, you can just eat a couple of popsicles!).
- Yarn (this works particularly well when you use a yarn that is multicolored—I used one that had all the quarter colors in it, but you can also choose a color that you particularly like).
- Markers or pens.

NOTES:
The God's Eye hanging totem (which originated with the Huichol Indigenous tribe) is a common decoration and craft project for children. When I came up with this idea for a workshop for the PantheaCon convention in 2008, I simply put a Pagan spin on a pre-existing craft. Keep this in mind if you come across other craft ideas that you like. Almost anything can become a witchy craft if you put the right slant on it. This craft in particular is a good example of how you can take a few very inexpensive supplies and make magick out of them.

MAGICKAL USES:
My original use for this project was as a Spring Equinox magickal working, although it could be used any time you want to make a new start.

DIRECTIONS:
- Begin by taking two popsicle sticks and a long strand of yarn. Wind the yarn around the sticks just enough to bind them together in a cross or X shape.

- Once they are tied together, take your pen or marker and write on the inner part of the X (the section that will eventually be covered by yarn) four things that you wish to be banished from your life or to lessen the influence of. For instance, you may write debt, over-eating, laziness, and insomnia. Whatever issues you want to let go of.
- Then, on the outer ends of the sticks (which will not be covered by yarn), write four things you wish to bring into your life in the days and months ahead. These would be such positive aspects as love, health, prosperity, and so on.
- Remember to concentrate on your intention to let go of the first four items and bring in the second four as you are doing the project.
- Once you are done writing, you will finish winding the yarn around the sticks in an over-and-under fashion (see diagrams) until you have covered the inner writing with yarn and formed a Goddess's Eye pattern. Leave the outer writing visible.

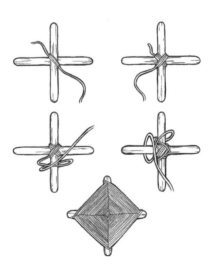

AFTERWARD:

- Hang your Goddess's Eye on your altar or wherever you will see it often to remind you of your intentions.

KNOT MAGICK ✶

SUPPLIES:

- Yarn or cord, anywhere from a foot to a yard long (any color will do, but you may wish to use a color that is associated with whatever you are doing magick for: green for prosperity, blue for health, pink or red for love, black for protection, and so on).

NOTES:

Knot magick is one of the oldest forms of magick that we know of and is often classified as "Women's Magick," since it was something that women could do unobtrusively and work into their embroidery, sewing, tapestry work, and other "women's chores" without being seen. It is still one of the simplest, least expensive, and most readily accessible of all magicks.

MAGICKAL USES:

Knot magick binds your spell or intention into a small and tangible form that can be easily tucked into a pocket or placed on an altar. It can be used for most forms of magickal work depending on the spell you use.

DIRECTIONS:

- One of the most common forms of knot magick is one that I discussed in my second book, *Everyday Witch A to Z*, and which is also referred to in many other magickal books.

- Take your piece of cord or yarn and tie nine knots in it, starting at the ends (knots #1 & #2), then the middle (#3), then halfway between the end knots and the middle knots (#4 & #5), then between the ends (#1 & 2) and the most recent knots (#4 & 5). Those knots will be #6 and #7.

- The last two knots (#8 & #9) will be between the central knot (#3) and the ones closest to it (#4 & #5).

- As you are tying your knots, visualize your magickal goal and recite the following traditional spell:

> *By the knot of one, the spell's begun.*
> *By the knot of two, it cometh true.*
> *By the knot of three, so mote it be.*
> *By the knot of four, open the door.*
> *By the knot of five, the spell's alive.*
> *By the knot of six, the spell is fixed.*
>
> *By the knot of seven, the stars of heaven.*
> *By the knot of eight, the stroke of fate.*
> *By the knot of nine, the thing is mine!*

AFTERWARD:

- Tuck your piece of cord or yarn in your pocket and carry it to remind you of your intentions and to bring the power of your spell with you. Or you can put it on your altar, in your wallet, or in a special spell box. When you are done with the spell, you can either undo the knots to release the spell or burn or bury the piece of yarn.

Easy Protection Magick *

Supplies:
- Black candle (white will do if you don't have black; you can tie a black string or cord around the bottom if you want to).
- Piece of black ribbon, string, or yarn (a black shoelace will work, in a pinch).
- Salt.
- Optional: sage smudge stick or incense.

Notes:
The easiest and cheapest form of this protection magick uses only the black string or cord. You can add the other elements if you feel a need for more serious protection or the first time you work the spell. Afterward, the yarn alone will be sufficient.

Magickal Uses:
Protection. This can be protection from harm from a person or persons or just general protection (for instance, when you are traveling).

Directions:
- This spell can be done at your altar or anywhere else you so desire. (If you are on the go and doing the spell in a hotel room or car, I'd skip the candle.)
- Place black string in a circle around your feet so you are standing inside the circle of string. Tie it closed once you are inside.
- Sprinkle the salt inside the yarn.
- If using sage, light the smudge stick or incense and let the smoke swirl around you in a circular

fashion and visualize it filling a cylinder-shaped
space around you.

- Light the candle (after putting the sage down
someplace safe or putting it out) and gaze at the
glow. In your mind, see the glow of the candle
spreading out to completely encompass your
body and say the following spell:

> *Cord of magick*
> *Filled with light*
> *Keep me safe*
> *Both day and night*

AFTERWARD:

- Once you're done, snuff out the candle and clear
away the salt. Step out of the string circle and
roll it up so you can carry it with you (you can
also wrap it around your wrist bracelet fashion,
or hang it around your neck, tucked out of sight
inside your clothes.

FABRIC

Poppet for Self-Improvement ✶ ✶

SUPPLIES:

- Piece of cloth (muslin or white cotton works
well, although you can use any bit of cloth you
have left over; you'll need a piece that is about 4
inches by 8 inches, although you can make your
poppet larger or smaller as desired).
- Needle and thread.
- Stuffing (you can use cotton balls, tissues, or
other small bits of cloth for this).
- Scissors.

- Marker.
- Small piece of paper or parchment.
- Pen.
- Optional: beads, yarn, herbs.

Notes:

Poppets are another traditional form of magick often used by women (although certainly not limited to women, by any means). Many Pagan cultures used poppets or dolls in one form or another; voodoo dolls are one obvious example, although these poppets have only a distant relation to them. The poppet is created by crafting a vaguely human-looking doll. The doll then stands for the person the spell is meant to affect; in this case, you.

Magickal Uses:

In this particular craft project, you will be creating a poppet for self-improvement (this will take a different slant for each person who does the spell, of course, depending on what each one feels needs improving). But it can also be used for healing or love magick, among other things. I don't recommend making a poppet that represents anyone other than yourself unless you have specific permission to do so (if someone requests you do healing magick for them, for instance). It is too easy to interfere with Free Will that way, and that's a no-no.

Directions:

- On your paper, write down a short list of things you want to improve about yourself or your life. Set it to the side but concentrate on those items as you create the doll.
- Draw an outline of your poppet on the cloth. If you fold the rectangle of cloth in half (so you have two square pieces attached at the top) you'll save yourself a little sewing. Or else

you can just outline the entire poppet and cut around all four sides. All you need is a simple human shape: head, neck, two arms, two legs, body.

- Once you've drawn the shape, cut it out with the scissors, and then sew it together. Start part of the way down one side; go down the leg, around the other leg, up the arm, over the head, and back down the other arm until you reach the side again. IMPORTANT: don't sew the poppet up completely until you have stuffed it. (You may find it easier to stuff each part as you go: first leg, second leg, first arm, head, second arm, and leave the body until last.) Don't worry about making nice neat stitches—your poppet doesn't have to be a work of art.

- Once you have sewn all but about two inches on the side, finish stuffing the inside of the poppet with whatever material you are using.

- Now is the time to add any herbs you might be using. For instance, if part of your self-improvement goal includes a healthier lifestyle, you might want to include a healing herb like calendula. If you want to try to relax more, add lavender. There is no right or wrong way to do this.

- Tuck your paper inside, and then finish sewing up the poppet.

- If you want to, you may decorate the doll so that it looks more like you; add eyes and mouth, draw in hair, or sew on some yarn of the appropriate color. Some people add beads (you can sew them on to any trouble spots to draw special attention there—if you want to become more open-hearted, for instance, you can sew a circle of beads over the heart area.) You can even make a little cloth outfit for your poppet if you are feeling particularly ambitious.

- Once the doll feels finished to you, you can say the following spell or one of your own:

Poppet, poppet
Me to you
Help me find
My path most true
Poppet, poppet
You to me
Help me reach
My destiny

AFTERWARD:

- Place the poppet someplace safe, such as an altar or a special box. If possible, put it someplace you can see it often, to remind you of your magickal working and your intention to follow through in the mundane world. But don't let this little doll get into anyone else's hands if you can help it.

Love Charm Bag ✳

SUPPLIES:
- Piece of cloth or pre-made fabric bag (muslin draw-string bags made for bath bags work well or little velveteen bags if you don't mind spending a couple of dollars more). Pink or red are the best colors for this project, but you can always use a white bag and just tie a pink or red ribbon around it.
- Needle and thread.
- One or more of the following herbs: rose buds or rose petals (fairly cheap if you can get them from the bulk section of a health food store, or free if you happen to grow roses—you can also buy a single rose for a buck or two at most grocery stores or florists), carnation (a very inexpensive flower if you don't want to pay for roses), clove, lavender, orange peel or orange blossoms, apple blossoms (if you happen to have an apple tree), cinnamon sticks.
- Ribbon or yarn.
- Optional: a piece of rose quartz or amethyst.

NOTES:
This is a variation on a love charm bag that I included in the New Moon ritual for May in *Circle, Coven & Grove*. Remember, when doing magickal work for love that it is better to do magick that is neutral (to open your own heart, for instance, or to bring love into your life) than magick that is specifically aimed at influencing another person (such as a love spell that is directed at a specific other). Not only will such a spell almost certainly interfere with Free Will, but it is likely to backfire when you least expect it. Seriously—take my word on this one.

Magickal Uses:

This charm bag is intended to attract love in general; that can mean romantic love, the love of friends or family, or even love from animal pals. If you cast an open-ended spell, it gives the gods room enough to send you the love you need, instead of the love you might think you want. If there is a specific type of love you feel is lacking in your life, you can certainly concentrate on that as you work on the charm bag.

Directions:

- If you are making your bag from scratch, cut out a piece of fabric that is about three inches wide by six inches long.
- Fold it in half so it is three by three, then sew up two of the open sides so you have a piece of fabric that is closed on three sides and open on one.
- It is more powerful to sew your own bag and place your intention with every stitch, but it is not completely necessary. If you don't feel like sewing, you can just cut out a circular piece of fabric, and close it later by tying a ribbon or string around it. Or you can just use a pre-made bag if you wish.
- Place the herbs you've chosen inside your bag along with the stone if you are using one.
- As you put each herb in the bag, concentrate on giving and receiving love and how that feels.
- Once the bag is filled, tie it shut with the ribbon or string, knotting the string three times while visualizing your desire.
- Recite this charm three times:

Love as a blessing
Love without harm
Love filled with sweetness
I call with this charm

AFTERWARD:
- Place the charm bag on your altar, underneath your pillow, or carry it with you. Don't forget to take it into your hands occasionally and squeeze it gently to release the aroma and power of the herbs.

Success Sachet ✳

SUPPLIES:
- Piece of cloth.
- Needle and thread.
- Herbs (try a combination of the following: basil, cinnamon, clove, ginger, nutmeg, peppermint, sandalwood, or spearmint—you'll notice that some of these are herbs you might commonly find in the kitchen cupboards).
- Optional: a piece of aventurine, bloodstone, malachite, tiger's eye, or turquoise (note that you can use a tumbled stone for this, then remove it when you are done with the sachet for reuse later in another magickal working).

NOTES:
If you are going into a particularly important situation, having a success sachet in your pocket can make you feel more relaxed and confident. That alone may help you succeed, although the magickal work certainly can't hurt!

MAGICKAL USES:
Success.

DIRECTIONS:
- Sew the fabric together on three sides, leaving one side open so you can put your herbs (and

stone, if using one) inside. Don't worry about how it looks; just make sure it is secure enough that the herbs won't leak out.

- As you sew each stitch, concentrate on your desire for success. Visualize the situation you will be going into as if you are there and see yourself glowing with self-confidence and strength.
- When you have sewn the three sides shut, put your herbs inside and sew the remaining side shut slowly and carefully.
- As you place each stitch, say out loud:
- I am divine, success is mine.

AFTERWARD:
- Tuck the sachet into your pocket or purse (preferably where you can touch it if you need to) before going into the situation you made it for. You can either keep it for later use or disassemble it once the need is over.

Protection Charm for the Home ✴

SUPPLIES:
- Piece of white cloth.
- Black or red ribbon or yarn.
- Rosemary and basil (dried is best).
- A clove of garlic.
- Some pins.
- Salt.
- Optional: an agate or red jasper stone.

NOTES:
This is another very simple use of magickal ingredients that many of us have around the house, all of them traditional. I like to use sea salt, but any kind will do.

Magickal Uses:
Protection of the home (or apartment), can also be used for cars if you change the charm a bit.

Directions:
- Cut a circular piece of cloth and lay the other charm ingredients in the center.
- Pull up the sides of the cloth to make a bundle then wrap the ribbon or yarn around it nine times to cinch it shut.
- Tie a knot to close it, and then tie eight more knots down the rest of the ribbon or yarn for a total of nine.
- As you are doing this, envision your home surrounded by a protective white light that emanates from the charm bundle. Say the following charm spell:

> *I make this charm*
> *Full of power*
> *To guard my home*
> *From this hour*

Afterward:
- Hang the charm bag up over the door used most often or in a corner that oversees the biggest space in the house.

HERBS AND PLANTS

Potpourri Scented Magick *

Supplies:
- Herbs (which ones will depend on what you are doing magick for).
- Water.

- Pot (preferably one you keep for this purpose) or simmerer.

NOTES:

Scent is the most powerful of all the five senses. It can affect the emotions, bring long-lost memories to the surface (remember mom's apple pie?), and carry magick on the very air we breathe. Simmering herbs on the stove or in a simmerer can spread the essence of your magickal working throughout your entire house with very little effort on your part. As a bonus, most herbs are fairly inexpensive!

MAGICKAL USES:

Any. If you want to do prosperity magick, use herbs that are specific to that kind of working, and the same goes for love, protection, or any other kind of magick. Here is a short (and not even close to complete) list of possible herb combinations for various simmering potpourri mixes. You'll note I mostly suggest ones that are cheap and readily available, although you can use some more exotic herbs if you don't mind paying for them. Try to use herbs with a strong scent for this type of magickal work.

- Love: lavender, cinnamon, lemon peel
- Healing: eucalyptus, peppermint, rosemary
- Prosperity: cloves, cinnamon, spearmint
- Protection: bay leaves, rosemary, sage
- Psychic Power/Intuition: chamomile, ginger, thyme

DIRECTIONS:
- Place the herbs in a pot of water on the stove and turn the heat up until it starts to simmer, then reduce the heat to as low as it can go. You can also use a simmering pot (they usually have little candles underneath) if you have one.

- If you are letting the herbs simmer for some time, you will eventually need to add more water.
- As you put each herb into the water, visualize the magickal work you are doing and your intention to spread that working out into the universe with the aroma from the simmering herbs.

AFTERWARD:

You may want to pour out the used herbs and water someplace special, such as a corner of your garden, outdoor circle, or under a tree.

A Witch's Herbal Broom ✳ ✳

SUPPLIES:

- Two-foot long stick or a fat dowel (if you can't find a stick), or any other length if you prefer.
- Broom straw (if you can find it).
- Various long, woody, aromatic herbs: cedar, lavender, lemon balm, rosemary, pine, and peppermint are some of my favorites.
- String.
- Scissors.
- Newspaper or cloth to protect the surface you're working on (bits and pieces of herbs will drop all over the place).
- Optional: colored ribbons.

NOTES:

Brooms are used for cleaning, so a Witch's broom is often used for spiritual or energetic purification. This is a great craft project for spring; you can then use the finished broom as a tool for giving your home a good energetic cleansing. If you don't have a garden or a yard full of shrubs, try looking at a local farmer's market, the flower section in the supermarket, or the florists. You may also be able to find dried herbs like this at craft stores. Alternately, if a friend or neighbor has any of these growing in their yard, you can always ask permission to clip a few pieces.

Magickal Uses:
Cleansing and purification.

Directions:
- Take your stick (or the dowel) and lay it down on the newspaper or cloth.
- Carefully choose pieces of herbs and trim them to the size you want. Lay them down in a bundle, piece by piece, making sure they fit together well and are visually pleasing.
- As you add each bit of herb, visualize it being filled with a powerful white light of purification. When you have your herbs arranged the way you want them, use the string to bind them to the stick (toward the bottom, so they look like a broom, of course).
- If you want, adorn your finished broom with pretty colored ribbons. (The quarter colors are nice for this, or any spring colors you like.)
- Either on the spot or in front of your altar, consecrate your magickal broom for purification by saying the following (or words of your choosing):

Magickal broom
Created with love
Sweep away trouble
With light from above
Sweep away sorrow
Sweep away strife
Bringing new power
And hope to my life

AFTERWARD:

- You can hang your broom on the wall by your altar for a while (it will eventually disintegrate, but should last for a few months), or take it outside and return its various components to the earth once it has done its job.

Yule Wreath ✶ ✶

SUPPLIES:

- Grapevine or willow for the wreath base, or a pre-made wreath base if you prefer not to make one. (I was given one by someone who bought it for a craft project and never got around to using it. Try keeping your eyes open for good craft supplies at yard sales and second-hand stores. Lots of people buy craft materials and then never use them.)
- Various decorative herbs and dried flowers (if you can find holly and mistletoe, they are the most appropriate for this project, and fresh pine or juniper springs are also great), natural items (pinecones, acorns, etc.).
- Ribbons in green, red, and/or gold.
- Marker.
- Lightweight wire (florist's wire works best and can be found in most craft sections).
- Optional: cinnamon sticks, cranberries, popcorn, glue gun.

NOTES:

This is a great project to do with friends (Pagan or otherwise). You can either do it as an early December craft project and hang it up for the rest of the season or save it for an icebreaker if you are having a holiday party. Because Christmas has such strong roots in the Pagan holiday of Yule, this is a magickal craft you can easily share with your non-witchy friends and family.

MAGICKAL USES:
Decoration and a celebration of the season.

DIRECTIONS:
- This project can be as simple or as complicated as you choose to make it.
- Create the wreath by twisting the base material in a circular shape and tying it with wire (or use a purchased wreath form if you prefer).
- Attach the various herbs, flowers, and other decorations by tucking them into the wreath, tying them on with wire, or gluing them on if necessary.
- A basic wreath may be nothing more than the wreath form, a bunch of pine boughs, and your ribbon. A fancier wreath may have five different kinds of herbs, beautiful flowers, pinecones, and a string of popcorn or cranberries wound around it. It is completely up to you.
- If you are working with a group of people, pass the wreath form around and let everyone take turns adding their own touches. Each person can take a piece of ribbon and write on it their wishes for the coming year, or what they are grateful for about the year that is ending.
- The ribbons can then be wound around the wreath or tied around the bottom of the wreath to hang down underneath.

Afterward:

- Hang your beautiful wreath up where you can see it. It can stay up until the Spring Equinox.

Magickal Oils ✶

Supplies:

- Various essential oils, which can include any of the following: basil, bergamot, calendula, chamomile, cinnamon, geranium, ginger, lavender, lemon, lemon balm, orange, peppermint, rose, rosemary, and special magickal oils such as High John the Conqueror.
- Base oils, which can include the following: almond, grapeseed, jojoba, olive, safflower, and sunflower. Be aware that some base oils turn rancid before others; I often use olive oil because I happen to have it in my kitchen, but it doesn't last as long. Jojoba, on the other hand, is more expensive but lasts for a very long time.

- Small glass jars or bottles with tops and droppers (some oils come with droppers in the covers, or you can re-use the droppers from children's medicines if you clean them well—otherwise, buy cheap droppers in the pharmacy section of a drug store).
- Paper and pen to make labels for your oils.
- Tape (to put the labels on with if you are not using pre-made labels that will stick).
- Optional: small funnel, sage or incense, salt and water, or other items for consecrating the oils once made.

NOTES:

Essential oils can vary dramatically in price and quality from company to company and depending on the plant used as the base. Rose and chamomile oils, for instance, are very pricy, while rosemary and lemon can be pretty cheap. I tend to buy tiny bottles of expensive oils and use less, but you can always leave those out altogether and use one of the other oils that have the same magickal qualities. My favorite brand of essential oils is a company called Nature's Alchemy, which I have found to be (amazingly) both the cheapest and the best quality. But there are many other brands out there that are also quite good. Just make sure that you are using essential oils (which are made, as the name would suggest, from the essence of real plants) and not fragrance oils, which are artificial, and therefore have no magickal qualities whatsoever. And remember that all these oils have medicinal qualities as well, and therefore can serve double duty in your house. Lavender, for instance, is wonderful for insomnia, bug bites, and burns, and will promote relaxation. I highly recommend getting a good book on essential oils, as well as one (or three) on the magickal uses of various plants and herbs. If you want to be frugal, start with just a few of the most all-around useful oils (such as lavender, rosemary, lemon, and peppermint) and expand your supplies slowly over time as you can afford to pick up a new one for your collection. Also, you only need to use a few drops at a time for most purposes, so you can buy very small amounts or share them with a friend.

MAGICKAL USES:
You can make up magickal oils for any and all forms of spellcasting. The oils can then be used in a variety of ways, including anointing (of candles, tools, spell parchment, or yourself), adding to bath water, and using in an oil diffuser. And once your magickal oil is made up, you only need to use a few drops each time, so it will last for ages. (Sometimes you have to weigh the initial expense of a magickal tool against how much use you will get out of it and the benefits of having it over time.) Here are some of the essential oils I use for my most common mixtures—remember that you can always vary a recipe to suit your own taste, fragrance preferences, and intuitive direction.

- Energy/Strength/Courage—cinnamon, ginger, lemon, orange
- Healing—calendula, lavender, lemon balm, rosemary
- Love—geranium, lavender, lemon, rose
- Peace/Happiness—bergamot, chamomile, geranium, lavender, lemon balm
- Prosperity—basil, bergamot, cinnamon, rosemary
- Protection/Purification—geranium, lemon, rosemary
- Psychic Ability/Conscious Mind—chamomile, ginger, lavender, peppermint

You will note that most of these essential oils have more than one magickal use. You may want to pick the uses you think you will most need and start with those oils.

DIRECTIONS:
- Mixing magickal oils is like a form of alchemy. You are taking neutral ingredients (the base oil or oils and the essential oils) and mixing them together with your intent and the force of your will to create a magickal oil. The process is quite simple; it is your will and intention that give it strength.
- On a clear space, such as the top of your altar or a kitchen counter, set out all your ingredients. Pour the base oil or oils you are using into a clean glass jar or bottle (you can reuse bottles from herb tinctures and such, just make sure to clean them completely with boiling water—and if you don't have a small funnel with which to pour the oils, try putting them into a measuring cup with a pouring lip first, or using a rolled up piece of stiff plastic). Leave a little space at the top.
- Carefully add your essential oils while focusing on your magickal purpose. I like to add the essential oil in combinations that add up to nine drops total because of the magickal significance of that number. So, if I were making love oil, for instance, I might use two drops each of geranium, lavender, and lemon, then only one drop of rose.
- Once you have all your oils in the bottle, cap it tightly and swirl the oils gently in a clockwise (deosil) direction nine times to mix them.

- If you want, you can chant the magickal purpose as you do for a little extra oomph. Then label your container and use as needed.

Afterward:
- I like to consecrate my magickal oils right after I make them—before I use them or put them away. But this is purely up to you. I store my magickal oils in the cabinet above my main altar to keep them separate from my non-magickal supplies. Some people have special boxes for theirs and I'll give instructions for making a suitable one later in this chapter. Here are a few of my favorite books on herbs and essential oils in case you want to add a resource or two to your collection.

Cunningham, Scott. *Cunningham's Encyclopedia of Magical Herbs.* St. Paul: Llewellyn, 1985.

—. *Magical Herbalism: The Secret Craft of the Wise.* St. Paul: Llewellyn, 1986.

Dugan, Ellen. *Cottage Witchery: Natural Magick for Hearth and Home.* St. Paul: Llewellyn, 2012.

Dunwich, Gerina. *The Wicca Garden: A Modern Witch's Book of Magickal and Enchanted Herbs and Plants.* New York: Citadel Press, 2018.

Morrison, Dorothy. *Bud, Blossom & Leaf: The Magical Herb Gardener's Handbook.* St. Paul: Llewellyn, 2001.

Wilson, Roberta. *Aromatherapy: Essential Oils for Vibrant Health and Beauty.* New York: Avery, 2002.

Worwood, Valerie Ann. *The Complete Book of Essential Oils & Aromatherapy.* San Rafael: New World Library, 2016.

Herbal Mixes for Protection, Love, & Health ✳

SUPPLIES:
- Various dried or fresh herbs and plants.
- Storage containers (preferably glass, not plastic) or cloth bags.
- Optional: mortar and pestle, knife or scissors.

NOTES:

As with the magickal oils above, herbal mixes are extremely simple to make. You simply gather the herbs you want to use (the lists of both herbs and resource books in the section above will work for this project as well), mix them together, add in your intention and magickal energy, then use them as you desire. Unlike essential oils, which must be purchased unless you want to go through the lengthy and difficult process of making them yourself, herbs and plants can easily come out of your own yard and garden, be gathered in wild fields or woods, purchased at farmer's markets, or even found in a grocery store. You can often find them for little or no money, which is a major advantage over the oils which can be more expensive. Some more specialized herbs may have to be ordered from Pagan sources or found in New Age or Pagan stores, but there are almost always cheaper substitutes you can use instead. And it is always preferred to grow your own magickal herbs if you have the space and inclination to do so. Even those with small apartments can grow a couple of herbs on a spare windowsill.

MAGICKAL USES:

Any. The only difference is that instead of using essential oils, you are working with dried or fresh plants. These will then be made into sachets, bath bags, and charm bags (like the love charm bag in the fabric section), stuffed into dream pillows, or placed in a bowl on your altar. There are virtually no limits to the uses you can find for herbal mixes, so it is nice to mix up a batch and have it on hand (in an airtight container) whenever you need it.

DIRECTIONS:
- Gather your herbs and plants together on a flat working surface. Herbs, especially once dried, will crumble and make a mess, so take that into consideration when choosing a place to work.
- Some types or forms of plants, like cinnamon sticks, tree bark, and other tougher herbs, may need to be ground up with a mortar and pestle. Others, like peppermint or chamomile, can be easily crumbled up between your fingers. Fresh herbs will have to be cut up (do not use an athame for this—either use a regular knife or a pair of scissors—herbs may be harvested using a special magickal knife called a boline, but I just use my regular garden clippers) or torn to pieces by hand.
- As you work, remember to concentrate on the magickal purpose the herbal mixture will be used for, and try to connect with the natural energy of the plants as you touch them.
- Mix together in whatever combination seems right to you. Try to pay attention to your instincts for which plants to add more or less of—there is no right or wrong way to do this.

AFTERWARD:
- Use your mixture immediately or store away for use in the future. Make sure that whatever container you use is airtight if you are making

a large batch to use over time. Herbs contain volatile oils that will eventually disappear over time, so you will have to replace most herbal mixtures every couple of years if you haven't used them up.

Healing Bath Bags ✳

SUPPLIES:
- Herbs (fresh or dried), including some of the following: calendula (marigold), eucalyptus, lavender, lemon balm, peppermint, rosemary, or any other healing herbs you prefer.
- Sea salt and/or Epsom salts.
- Muslin drawstring bag or any piece of thin white cotton cloth with ribbon or string to bind it closed.
- Optional: oatmeal.

NOTES:
This project was first included in my book, Circle, Coven & Grove: A Year of Magickal Practice, under the September Full Moon section, but it can be done any time you feel the need for a little extra healing.

MAGICKAL USES:
Healing (although you can, of course, make magickal bath bags for prosperity, protection, love, or any other use simply by substituting other herbs and altering your intention).

DIRECTIONS:
- Mix together the herbs and the salt (and oatmeal if you are using it). As you are combining the ingredients, visualize them being filled with a blue or yellow healing light.

- Place about three tablespoons of the mixture into the muslin bag or put it into the center of the piece of cloth and tie it closed. Hold the bag in your hands, close your eyes, and spend a few minutes directing healing energy into the bath bag.
- Then recite the following spell, or your own if you have one:

> *I am love and strength*
> *Energy and power*
> *My health improves*
> *With every hour*

AFTERWARD:
- Use the bath bag by floating it in a tub of water while you bathe or scrub your skin gently with it in the shower. Remember to visualize the healing light moving out of the bag and into you as you do so.

Corn Dollies ✸ ✸

SUPPLIES:
- Husk from corn on the cob.
- String.
- Something to stuff the doll with (cotton balls or tissues work).

NOTES:
Corn dollies are a traditional craft usually made around the time of Mabon, the Autumnal Equinox. They celebrate the importance of corn and other grains in earlier Pagan cultures and symbolize the sacrifice that comes with the harvest. There are many different ways to make corn

dollies; this happens to be one of the simplest. (According to some folks, the original corn dollies weren't made with corn at all, but with wheat. But this project uses corn.)

MAGICKAL USES:
Celebration of the harvest season.

DIRECTIONS:
- Husk an ear or two of corn and save the husks (outer leaves). Feel free to eat the corn!
- Using the largest outer leaves, fold the leaves over your stuffing material to form a head.
- Tie a piece of string around the neck area, leaving the husks underneath loose, as if in a doll's skirt.
- Take a few of the smaller husks and tie them across the body of the doll to act as arms. (A crisscross or figure eight motion should secure the arms reasonably well.)
- This is your corn dolly. If you want, you can add herbs or flowers as decorations.

AFTERWARD:
- There are two different choices for what to do with your corn dolly once it is formed. You can place it on your altar or hang it up somewhere in your house until next year when you will replace it with a new one. Or you can throw it into your Mabon bonfire, should you have one, to symbolize the sacrifice that comes with the bounty of the harvest. If you choose the second approach, you can also take a slip of paper and write on it those things that you are willing to sacrifice for a successful harvest in your life (bad habits, perhaps, or parts of your life that

no longer work for you). Tuck the paper into the corn dolly before throwing it onto the fire and let the smoke from the flames send your intention out into the universe.

Wheel of the Year ✶ ✶ ✶

SUPPLIES:
- Long pieces of straw, wheat, or any flexible plant (grapevine, for instance). The plant should be flexible enough to bend and shape, but also dry enough to burn when thrown on a bonfire. Branches of various trees will work as well, but they have to be dry enough to burn but still flexible enough to move around.
- Twine or string.
- Optional: paper and pen, various herbs such as rosemary or sage.

NOTES:
This looks like an easy project, and in theory, it is. But it can also be quite tricky to find the right kind of plant matter and work it into the shape you want. It can be much easier to do if you have more than one person working on the project at a time—at least one person to bend the straw, vine, or branches into shape, and another to tie them into place.

Having at least three people works even better, so this is a great project for a coven or any other gathering of Witches.

MAGICKAL USES:
Celebration of the Wheel of the Year, usually at one of the three harvest festivals: Litha, Mabon, or Samhain.

DIRECTIONS:
- Your goal is to form a Wheel of the Year; a circle with eight spokes on the inside, radiating out from the center, to symbolize the eight Sabbats that make up the Pagan Wheel of the Year.
- Take a large branch or swath of wheat, or whatever material you are using, and tie it into a circular shape. This should be reasonably sturdy but doesn't have to be very thick.
- Take two pieces of material and tie them together in a cross shape—this will give you four of the spokes. Repeat this with another two pieces and join all four together to get eight spokes.
- Place these in the middle of your circle and tie the ends to the outer circle. This will give you a Wheel with eight spokes.
- If you want, decorate the Wheel with bits of herbs or flowers.

AFTERWARD:
- It seems almost a pity to do it, after all the hard work to make it, but the Wheel of the Year is created to be destroyed in a bonfire celebrating the harvest. It can be used at any harvest holiday, but I like to use it at Samhain when we say goodbye to the old year and welcome in the new. If you want, you can write your wishes for the year to come on slips of paper and tuck them into the Wheel of the Year before throwing it onto the fire.

WOOD

Tarot Card/Spell Box ✶

SUPPLIES:
- Wooden box.
- Decorations (these can include shells, rocks, leaves, beads, pictures, or anything else that appeals to you).
- Glue.
- Optional: wood-burning tool, hot glue gun, paint, markers.

NOTES:

You can often buy inexpensive wooden boxes new through Pagan stores or craft stores, but I think it is more fun for this project to hunt for the perfect old box. Try looking at yard sales, second-hand stores, thrift stores, or anyplace else where someone else's trash can become your treasure. Before you look for a box, you will probably want to decide what you want to use it for, so you get one that is the right size. A standard deck of tarot cards, for instance, will fit in a smaller box than you would need if you wanted to store all your magickal supplies. But if you want a spell box (one which only needs to hold the elements for a spell, such as a few herbs, a stone or two, and maybe a piece of parchment paper), you might be able to get away with something fairly tiny.

MAGICKAL USES:

Your box can be used to hold tarot cards or rune stones, the ingredients for one spell or many, or the magickal oils you made from the instructions earlier in this chapter. Or you can make a box that is large enough to hold all your magickal supplies or your Book of Shadows. It is all up to you.

DIRECTIONS:
- Depending on your taste and your crafting skills, this box can be either plain and simple or very elaborate.
- Gather whatever decorations you plan to use and lay them out on top (and on the sides if you are decorating the entire box) before starting to apply them. If you are going to have a central symbol, such as a pentacle or a moon, you may want to sketch it out first before painting, drawing, or wood-burning it.
- Work slowly and carefully, being mindful of the fact that you are crafting a box to hold something (or somethings) precious. You can use a single medium (only leaves, for instance, or only paint), or you can mix up a number of different types of decoration. Maybe you want to use shells to represent Water, stones for Earth, feathers for Air, and so on. If you are going to use the box to hold tarot cards, you can trace the picture of your favorite card (or The Fool, since he is first) on the top of the box.
- If the box will be used to hold the ingredients for a particular spell, you will want to suit the decorations to your magickal intent. For instance, a box made to hold a spell for love might have hearts, roses, symbols for male and female (or whichever ones are appropriate for your desires), pictures of images you consider romantic, and the like. The box doesn't have to be a work of art; it just has to suit the needs and tastes of the one who created it.

AFTERWARD:
- Before using your box for the first time, you may wish to bless and consecrate it for magickal use. Then place your cards, spell ingredients, or tools inside it. And if you want, make another for a witchy friend and give it as a gift.

Speaking Stick for Circle Harmony ✴ ✴

SUPPLIES:
- A stick (a foot long or a bit longer and about an inch around; if you don't have any trees in or around where you live, then try going for a walk in a park or other wooded area).
- Lengths of colored ribbon.
- Various decorations such as feathers, shells, beads, etc.
- Sting or thread.
- Optional: wood-burning tool, leather thong, a crystal point, glue, markers, silver or copper wire.

NOTES:
If you have ever practiced with a coven or group, you have probably seen the practice of passing a speaking stick at the end of a ritual. Once the main ritual is over, usually after "Cakes and Ale" have been passed, the speaking stick is sent around the circle. Each person gets a chance to speak their thoughts without interruption from others, and all the focus of the circle is devoted at that moment to the one who is speaking. This is a powerful tool, this stick. And it can be helpful in keeping harmony in an ongoing group practice since it ensures that everyone will have a chance to speak and be heard. So, this is a perfect project for a coven or circle to do together, whether they are just starting to practice together or have been doing so for years.

MAGICKAL USES:
Circle harmony and personal empowerment.

DIRECTIONS:
- Each person in the group should bring an object with them to add to the stick. This can be a feather, a personal totem, a few beads, or anything else that has meaning to them. Found objects are fine—no need to go out and buy something expensive.
- They should also each choose a piece of ribbon in whichever color appeals to them. Pass the stick around the circle and have each person add their own touches and tie on a ribbon. When Blue Moon Circle did this project, we each wrote on our ribbon something we liked about the others or the group as a whole. We also each took a marker and drew a symbol or symbols and added our personal bits as well.
- If you want to add a crystal point at the top, it can be done, although it is a bit tricky. You may want to carve out an indentation that the crystal will fit into in order to stabilize it. Then you can attach it with copper or silver wire, or a piece of damp leather thong (the leather will tighten as it dries, but unless your point is exactly the right shape, this can be hard to get to stay on correctly).
- You can also add a string of beads, with each person contributing a bead that stands for their presence in the group. As you pass the stick around and each person takes turns decorating it, you may want to talk about what it is about the group that touches you spiritually or helps you with your magickal life.

- When the speaking stick is finished, do a blessing or consecration of your new tool together.

AFTERWARD:
- Use your speaking stick at the end of each ritual; not only to give each one in the group a chance to be heard, but also to remind you of what you can achieve when you work (and play) together.

The Magick Wand ✳

SUPPLIES:
- A piece of wood.
- Any decorations you choose (if you want them at all).
- Optional: markers, wood-burning tool, paint, carving tools, quartz or amethyst crystal, silver or copper wire, sharp knife.

NOTES:
This is another project that can be as simple or as ornate as your taste and skill-level dictate. Someone who is a skilled woodcarver, for instance, may choose to decorate their wand with flowing arcane symbols. Another Witch may prefer to draw or paint their wand with the four quarter colors or the shapes of the changing moon. Yet another Witch might rather have a plain wooden wand with only a simple crystal bound to the top with silver wire. The wand is a very personal tool, so be sure to make one that suits your own style. And there is nothing wrong with walking through the woods until you find the perfect piece of wood and using it just as it is.

MAGICKAL USES:
Directing energy or occasionally stirring.

DIRECTIONS:

- The instructions for making a wand are much like those above for making a speaking stick but without ribbons or dangling ornamentation.
- If you want to, you can draw, paint, carve, or wood-burn any symbols you like; some favorites are the phases of the moon, the sun, stars, pentacles, rune signs, your magickal name or symbol, or any symbols particular to your own path or practice. (For instance, those following a Celtic path would use Celtic symbols, and those who follow an Egyptian path would use different ones.)
- If you want to have a crystal on top, either a clear quartz crystal or an amethyst is usually used (the quartz ones are much cheaper, of course), but you can also just use any pretty rock that appeals to you. Try winding some copper or silver wire around it to hold the stone in place. Copper wire can be found fairly cheaply at hardware stores.
- Or simply find a stick of a size and shape that appeals to you, and trim it slightly until it fits your hand perfectly and the balance feels right.

AFTERWARD:

- If you like, bless and consecrate your new wand on the first Full Moon after you've made it. Then keep it on your altar or in some other safe and sacred place.

PAPER

Parchment Spell Paper ✶

SUPPLIES:
- White paper (something a little thicker than printer paper if you have it, although regular paper will work).
- Cold coffee or tea.
- Blow-dryer.
- Pan or deep plate.
- Optional: pens or markers, ribbon.

NOTES:
Spells look beautiful and magickal when you write them out on parchment paper. And you can spend quite a bit on individual sheets of parchment paper if you buy them from a Pagan store (although they usually come all rolled up with a lovely ribbon, which is nice). Luckily, there is a cheap and simple way to make parchment paper at home with things that you are likely to already have in your kitchen.

MAGICKAL USES:
Paper for writing special spells on.

DIRECTIONS:
- Rip the edges of your paper carefully by hand so they are ragged (if you use scissors, you won't get the same effect).
- If you want the paper to look even more authentic, crumple it up, then smooth it out again.
- Soak the paper on a cookie sheet, pan, or deep plate in either coffee or tea and leave it to sit for about five minutes. It should be darker when you take it out than it was when it went in.

- Pour off all the liquid and dry the paper with the blow-dryer for another five minutes or until it is no longer damp. (Traditionally, this was accomplished by putting the paper in the oven to dry on low, but that makes me a bit nervous …)
- If you want, you can decorate the edges with drawings or symbols and tie it up with a ribbon until you are ready to use it.

AFTERWARD:
- When you have a special spell that you want to write out by hand, use the paper you made yourself, and take advantage of the magickal energy you have already put into it.

Homemade Herbal Paper ✹ ✹ ✹

SUPPLIES:
- Scrap paper (you can use any kind of paper for this from computer paper to newspaper, just be aware that paper with dark inks in it will turn your final homemade paper gray).
- Stapler or staple gun.
- A wooden frame the size of the paper you want to make (an old picture frame with the glass taken out will do).
- Window screening (slightly larger than the frame).
- Large plastic tub (that screen will fit in).
- Blender.
- Felt or wool fabric (slightly larger than the frame).
- Sponge.
- Herbs.
- Flowers or seeds.
- Optional: dryer lint (helps make paper stronger), corn starch, rolling pin.

Notes:

This is a great craft to do as a group or with your kids. It combines recycling with creativity, turning old scrap paper into beautiful herb-infused paper you made yourself.

Magickal Uses:

Paper for spell-writing, making into a journal or a Book of Shadows, gift wrapping for Yule.

Directions:

- Tear old paper into small pieces. Soak the pieces for a few hours or overnight (this will start to break down the fibers, so they are easier to mash up in the blender).
- Place in blender with water, about a cup of paper to two or three cups of water. Blend until it turns into a light mush, like watery oatmeal.
- If you plan to write on your paper, you may want to add a tablespoon or so of cornstarch or the dryer lint. These will help your paper hold together better and absorb less ink.
- When the paper mash is ready, add in whichever herbs, flowers, or seeds you like and mix briefly. If you want the flowers to be whole, add them later.
- Make a mold by stapling the screen over the wooden frame.
- Put about two inches of water into your plastic tub and mix the blender of paper mush into it.
- Dip your screen mold into the tub at an angle and pick up as much mush with it as you can. You can help spread it with your hands if you want to. When you have a layer on your mold, tilt it so the water runs off, then carefully blot as much water as you can with a cloth or paper towel.

- Cover your mold with a piece of felt cloth and gently turn it over onto a flat surface (the water will run off through the cloth).
- Carefully peel your paper off onto the felt. (It may just come off when you tap it, or you may need to dry it a bit more.) If you want to add whole flowers, herbs, or seeds, you can do so now and press them into your paper with a rolling pin or any heavy object.
- You can help the paper dry faster and flatter by placing newspapers, a cookie sheet, or another heavy flat object on top.

AFTERWARD:

- When your paper is dry, peel it off the felt slowly and carefully. It can be used for numerous spell applications, but one of my favorites is to write a spell on a paper that has seeds imbedded in it (and perhaps herbs that are good for that particular magickal working), and then bury the paper after you have cast the spell. As the seeds bloom, they will carry your magickal intent to the surface.

Decorating a Book of Shadows ✶ ✶

SUPPLIES:

- Pre-existing Book of Shadows or any nice notebook or journal.
- Leaves or dried flowers.
- Colored or foil papers.
- Ribbon.
- Cut-out pictures or drawings (these will be the decorations, so pick out items that have meaning to you or that you think will be the

most appropriate as the cover of your Book of Shadows).

- Decoupage glue or white glue that has been slightly thinned out.
- A popsicle stick or other flat object (for smoothing out wrinkles).
- Foam brush or regular brush (for spreading out glue).
- A damp rag.
- Optional: scissors, tweezers (to help with positioning), glitter.

Magickal Uses:

A Book of Shadows is used to write down spells and rituals, keep track of dreams, mark down magickal progress, and generally chronicle a Witch's magickal life.

Directions:

- Lay out your decorations on the top of your Book of Shadows until you get them the way you want them.
- One piece at a time, remove the decoration and spread a small amount of glue on the book or on the back of the item, and press it gently into place. It is okay if items overlap.
- Once all the pieces are glued down, apply a thin layer of glue on top. If you want to add glitter, now's the time to do so. Let each layer of glue dry, then add additional layers until you have the effect you want.
- Make sure the outer edges are smooth, so they won't catch on anything later.

Afterward:

- Place all your favorite spells and rituals inside and keep in a special place or on your altar.

Homemade Tarot Cards ✶ ✶ ✶

SUPPLIES:
- Thick paper (card stock works well, you will need 20 sheets if you are making the 78 standard-sized cards, or fewer if you are making smaller cards).
- Colored pens and markers.
- Cut out pictures or photos.
- Scissors or paper cutter.
- Optional: glue, laminating paper.

NOTES:
The easiest way to make your own tarot cards is to copy the original cards (usually the Rider-Waite deck) from an online site and print them out with your printer. But frankly, if you're going to do that, I think you might as well just spend the fifteen or twenty dollars and buy your own deck. If you use them often, it will probably be worth it. On the other hand, you can create a deck that is truly your own with just a little more time and effort. And who knows: your own deck might just work for you better than any store-bought cards could.

MAGICKAL USES:
Divination and clarification of life issues.

DIRECTIONS:
- Cut your paper into equal-sized rectangles of whatever size you prefer. You can make them over-sized like regular tarot cards, the size of playing cards, or even make a mini deck that is easier to carry with you.
- If you are going to make a standard deck, you will want to have 78 cards: 22 major arcana cards, and 56 minor arcana cards divided into

four suits. The suits are usually wands or staffs, cups, swords, and pentacles, but you can certainly use different symbols if you choose to. It is easier, however, to base your cards on the original deck unless you are a truly creative and artistic type.

- For each card, you will draw a picture or glue on pictures (or photographs) you have found elsewhere. For instance, for the Queen of Cups, you may want to use a picture or a photo of a beautiful woman. Or you may draw a simple picture of a woman wearing a crown and holding a cup. If your artistic skills are limited, you could always just draw a cup with a crown over it.

- Let your imagination and your instincts run wild here since you will be using these cards later to channel your own inner wisdom as well as information you might get from outside sources. For instance, The Tower card (a symbol of chaos and destruction) could be a drawing of a broken tower, or a picture of the Twin Towers after 9/11.

- If this seems like an overwhelming task, start with just a few cards, or just the major arcana and add the rest later on.

- Here are a couple of basic books on tarot that might help you to figure out what you want to put on your cards, as well as how to interpret them later. One is a very old approach and the other is more modern.

Greer, Mary K. *Tarot for Your Self: A Workbook for Personal Transformation*. Newburyport: Weiser Books, 2019.

Waite, Arthur Edward. *The Pictorial Key to the Tarot*. Stamford: U.S. Games Systems, 1997. (Originally published in 1910.)

AFTERWARD:
- You may want to keep your cards in a special box (such as the one described earlier in this chapter) or a drawstring pouch. If you used a lot of photographs or glued-on pictures that might come loose over time, you may want to consider laminating them when you are done.

GLASS

A Witch's Bottle ＊

SUPPLIES:
- A small glass bottle or jar.
- A lid or a cork for sealing the bottle.
- Salt.
- Dried basil.
- Dried rosemary or juniper.
- A clove of garlic.
- Pins.
- Optional: a tumbled agate or red jasper stone or a few jasper or agate beads, sealing wax.

NOTES:
Witch's bottles were originally designed to protect against Witches (imagine that), but these days when we talk about a Witch's bottle, it is usually a form of protection magick. Various protective items are placed in a bottle or jar, which is often buried or hidden. When I moved into my new home (many years ago now), I made a Witch's bottle and buried it in front of the door I use as the main entrance to the house.

MAGICKAL USES:
Protection.

DIRECTIONS:
- Take the bottle or jar and place all your protective items in it.
- Put on the lid, if it has one, or place a cork in the top. If you want to make it even fancier, you can use sealing wax to secure the cork or lid in place.
- If you want, say a protection spell or this charm:

I make this bottle
Full of power
To protect this home
From this hour

AFTERWARD:
- Bury the bottle near your front door. If you can't bury it, you can hide it right outside or inside the door.

Decorating a Glass Chalice ✶

SUPPLIES:
- Inexpensive glass goblets (you can get these at the dollar store or find them at flea markets).
- Glass paints or markers (from a craft shop, about five to ten dollars).

NOTES:
This is a simple way to create a ritual chalice for yourself or a group without spending a lot of money. If you are working as a group, everyone should take turns adding their individual touches to the goblet.

MAGICKAL USES:
Ritual chalice for Cakes and Ale or pouring libations to the gods.

DIRECTIONS:
- Use the glass paints or markers to draw symbols such as moons, pentacles, snakes, grapes or other plants or vines, Celtic symbols, rune signs, etc. on the glass.

AFTERWARD:
- Be careful when cleaning the glass. The paints or markers should stand up to light cleaning but should not be put through the dishwasher. Only use your ritual goblet for magickal purposes, never for casual drinking.

A Scrying Mirror ✶

SUPPLIES:
- Round mirror (if you can't find a round mirror with a wood frame, you can always get a round picture frame and put glass into it. But that makes the project a bit more difficult).
- Black glass paint (regular paint will peel off) or glossy black fingernail polish (you can usually find bottles of cheap polish for a few dollars).
- Glue.
- Decorations for around the edges, such as shells, stones, beads, etc.

NOTES:
Scrying mirrors are another form of divination or seeing beyond that which is normally available to us in the mundane world. They are usually black glass or some other reflective surface.

MAGICKAL USES:
Divination.

Directions:

- Paint the mirror with your black paint or black fingernail polish. Be careful around the edges, unless you want them to be black, too.
- If you are using a mirror with a wooden frame, you can either leave it as is or paint it black as well. Plastic frames are difficult to both paint and glue on and I don't recommend them.
- Once the mirror has dried, glue your decorations around the edges.

Afterward:

- Use your scrying mirror in a dim room with candles around you if possible. Look into the darkness and see what appears.

STONE

Gemstone Necklace ✶ ✶

Supplies:

- Various gemstone beads, as many or as few as you want to use. You can often find old strings of beads at thrift stores or yard sales for not very much or buy a few beads at a craft store. For reasonably priced beading supplies, try firemountaingems.com.
- If you want a variety of beads, try going in on a few different kinds with some friends, so you can share the expense.
- Beading wire, fishing line, thin leather thong, satin cord, or a thin metal chain. Keep in mind

that if you are using a thicker material, like leather, you will need to get beads with bigger holes. I don't recommend using sewing thread since it almost always breaks eventually, as the rough edges inside the beads rub against it over time.

- Optional: glass beads, silver or silver-plated beads (to use as inexpensive spacers), clasps and crimp beads, needle nose pliers

Notes:

I make jewelry for a living (well, part of one), so this craft is second nature to me. And beadwork is fairly easy to do if you have any experience with it at all. If you are just starting out, you may want to keep your necklace pretty simple—put the beads on a length of clear fishing line or skinny satin cord (if you can find beads with holes large enough to fit over it), tie a knot in it, and be done.

The purpose here is focused on creating a necklace to wear when doing magick, so don't worry if it isn't perfect. Pick stones that resonate with you or relate to the magick you are going to be doing. My two favorite reference books for magickal work with stones are:

Cunningham, Scott. *Cunningham's Encyclopedia of Crystal, Gem & Metal Magic (Second Edition)*. St. Paul: Llewellyn, 2011.

Chase, Pamela Louise, and Jonathan Pawlik. *Healing with Gemstones*. Franklin Lakes: New Page, 2002.

Magickal Uses:

Boosting power and intent of spellwork of any kind. Connection with the earth. Grounding.

DIRECTIONS:

- If you are creating a necklace to be used with one specific type of spell (such as love or prosperity), you may want to pick stones that resonate particularly well with that goal. For instance, all green stones work well for prosperity magick, black onyx and red jasper are good for protection, and so on. You can rely on books for correspondence information, or simply go with your gut feelings. (And your wallet, of course—not everyone can afford to get tourmaline, no matter how powerful it might be.)
- If you want to make a traditional Witch's necklace, you can use amber and jet (you can get jet from the site listed above, although it is otherwise sometimes tough to find). You don't have to use a lot of any one kind of bead, either.
- String your beads on your wire, thong, or whatever material you are using.
- If you don't want to mess around with clasps, remember to use something that will knot easily and stay knotted, and make your necklace long enough to go over your head. Otherwise, place a crimp bead on each end, thread your wire ends through the clasp and back out again, and crimp the crimp bead tightly with the pliers.
- Make sure there are no rough bits of metal that will scratch your neck. If necessary, crunch the crimp beads up a bit more, making sure they are secure on the end of your wire and won't pull loose.

AFTERWARD:

- If you want, bless and consecrate your necklace for magickal work and wear it when you are casting a spell or doing any form of ritual. Keep it with your spell supplies, not your jewelry, if you can.

Simple Stone Magick *

SUPPLIES:
- A tumbled gemstone or a crystal (if you don't want to spend money on one of these, a simple rock from the beach or yard will do, as long as you take the trouble to find one that seems "special" to you.)
- Optional: magickal oil (such as the ones discussed earlier in this chapter), salt, sage, a small bag or box

NOTES:
This isn't really a craft, per se, since you don't do a whole lot to the stone you have chosen. In truth, much of the "craft" is in the choosing. When you are searching for a stone to do this task with, make sure you look for one which seems to call to you in some way.

MAGICKAL USES:
Whichever one you choose. But make sure you know which magickal working you'll be doing before you go looking for the stone, so your intuition will lead you to the right one for that particular spell or ritual.

DIRECTIONS:
- Decide what you will be doing spellwork for, and search for just the right stone.
- Once you have found it, create sacred space in a circle or in front of your altar. Take the stone in one hand and simply hold it for a few minutes, concentrating on creating a bond between you and the natural energy of the rock.
- Turn to the North and say, "I thank you, powers of Earth, for granting me this stone for my work. I will value it as the symbol of your power and use its strength only for good."

- If you want, you can also dab it with the appropriate magickal oil, sprinkle a little salt on it, and waft some sage over it. The stone is now ready to be used for your magickal task.

AFTERWARD:
- Put the stone on your altar or place it in a special box or bag with your other magickal tools.

Stone Scrying ✶

SUPPLIES:
- All you need for this craft is a space outside where you have room to walk and there are a number of stones scattered around. Almost any yard, park, or woods will do.

NOTES:
Like the stone magick above, this isn't really a craft. But it is a good example of how you can take items that are already in your environment (and completely free) and turn them into a magickal tool.

MAGICKAL USES:
Divination.

DIRECTIONS:
- My friend Caere (a Pagan and a shaman, as well as a terrific professional hypnotherapist) taught me this magickal trick.
- Go outside to a place where there are stones lying around on the ground.
- Close your eyes for a moment and concentrate on a question you would like the answer to.
- Then open your eyes and VERY CAREFULLY walk backward until an inner voice tells you to stop.

- Look down and pick up the first rock you spot. Take the rock and look at it—see if you can see any patterns or pictures in the rock that pertain to your question. (This may sound strange—but I've done it, and I assure you, it really works!)

AFTERWARD:
- Put the rock on your altar for a while and pick it up occasionally to see if there is something you missed the first time.

A note on blessing and consecrating new magickal tools: As you've seen, I often recommend consecrating a new tool for magickal use. Is this absolutely necessary? No, it isn't. But it can be a meaningful addition to the creation of the item and it lends an extra magickal "oomph" to your tool. Blessing and consecrating a magickal object gives it a bit more power since you are focusing your intent and taking it one step further.

Consecrating a new tool is fairly simple and can be done in any number of ways. I usually bring the tool into sacred space (if I'm not already working in a circle while making the object) and call in the powers of the four quarters. I bless the object with the four elements (usually water, salt, a feather or incense for Air, and a candle flame for Fire) and state out loud that I am dedicating it to positive and magickal use. I ask the God and Goddess to bless the object and its wielder (me). And that's that.

But now the tool is dedicated to magickal use and cleansed of any unnecessary or negative energy, and it is ready to be put to work when next I need it. You can add this step to any of the crafts in this chapter if you so desire.

CHAPTER 6

FEEDING THE MASSES: FORTY-FIVE FEAST DISHES FOR LESS

One of my favorite parts of Pagan celebrations, I must admit, is the feasting. When Blue Moon Circle gathers together for the Sabbats, we usually start with a ritual and follow up with a feast. Everyone brings a dish (or two) to pass; usually, there are friends and family there as well, and the food is both abundant and very, very good.

What's more, it is usually pretty inexpensive as well.

You see, I may not have mentioned one little thing about the women of Blue Moon Circle—we're all kinda cheap. Let's say "frugal"…it sounds better. But the truth is, none of us has a lot of extra money. Many of the ladies have families to feed, too. So, we've all learned to make our food dollars stretch as far as possible while still putting healthy, delicious, and interesting meals on the table.

And that goes for the feast table as well.

Hence this chapter. Almost all the recipes here have made an appearance on one Blue Moon Circle feast table or another, and some are old favorites that we serve over and over again. And they can all be made for about ten dollars or less, assuming you are trying to feed a reasonably sized group and that everyone will be contributing a dish to pass. (The point of feast food is that everyone brings something, so no one has to make a huge amount of food or spend a huge amount of money.)

Food prices vary, of course. The cost of your ingredients can depend on a lot of variables: where you live, what time of year it is, whether or not the item is grown locally, what the economy is doing, and so on.

But there are some ways to make your food dollar stretch further, despite these issues. For instance, if you have the space and the inclination, you can grow some of your food yourself. I have a large garden, and for much of the year, my contribution to the feast table is based predominantly on what happens to be ripe in my garden at the time. These dishes cost me little or nothing and have the additional benefit of being organic and full of the positive energy I put into growing their ingredients.

Not everyone has a garden, of course. But you can try the next best thing, which is to buy your feast food from a local gardener, farm stand store, or farmer's market. Local foods tend to be cheaper, fresher, and often have fewer pesticides and preservatives since they don't have to survive week-long trips across the country to get them to their consumers.

If you don't want to go to the trouble of having a garden or live in a place where that isn't a choice, you may want to consider joining a CSA (community-supported agriculture or crop-sharing system). This is a great alternative to growing your own food, which still allows you to get fresh, in-season produce while also supporting local farmers.

The way these work is simple—you sign up with a local grower for a season and pay a certain amount every month (usually much less than you would pay for the same amount of produce from a grocery store). In return, you get a weekly delivery of whatever is in season at the moment. In the spring, this usually means lots of greens, maybe some strawberries and herbs as well. Later in the season, you will get a basket overflowing with tomatoes, squash, and whatever else is abundant.

There are a few possible drawbacks to this arrangement: you are limited to whatever the farmer has growing at the moment, and may therefore sometimes end up with veggies you don't much like. (On the positive side, you will probably end up developing a taste for food you never would have tried, otherwise.) Sometimes, you have to go to the farm to pick up your produce instead of having it delivered. And if nature is unkind, you suffer the side-effects along with the grower.

Still, I have known many people who have gone this route, and every one of them has been wildly enthusiastic about the results and signed up for another year. If you can't have a garden of your own, this is the next best thing to doing so. (Some CSA farms will even allow you to trade labor for some of the cost of your food if you are willing to get your hands dirty.)

What if you can't grow your own food and don't have access to either a CSA or a local farmer's market? Or it is the depths of winter, and no one is growing anything except calluses from shoveling?

There are also a number of ways to save money at the grocery store, so buying your feast food doesn't mean going without milk and bread for the rest of the week. Blue Moon Circle folks often do one or more of the following:

USE COUPONS AND TAKE ADVANTAGE OF STORE SPECIALS. Now that the economy is a little more challenging, coupon clipping is making a come-back. Blue Mooner Jhaea is a pro; she has been known to buy a hundred dollars' worth of groceries and only spend about twelve dollars. Frankly, I'm just not that good. But if I check to see what I have coupons for, I can sometimes pick a feast recipe that costs me a lot less than it might have if I hadn't gotten the main ingredient for half off.

BUY IN BULK. If you use an ingredient often, or you will be cooking for a group of people, buying in bulk can often save you a lot of money. Be sure to double-check the cost per pound (or gallon, or whatever) to make sure that the bigger container is really a deal, though. (Stores that specialize in selling bulk foods are often a good option if you can use up the larger containers before they go bad.)

LOOK FOR SALES. If you were thinking of making chicken for your feast dish but the store is having a sale on turkey breasts, you may want to alter your recipe to take advantage of the sale item. The same principle applies to fruits and vegetables. And sometimes seeing what's on sale will even give you an idea of what to make. Look for "buy one, get one free" specials when you are trying to decide what to cook since that would mean half the ingredients are free.

BUY MEAT THAT IS ALMOST AT ITS SELL-BY DATE. If you look in the meat department, you will often see meat that has a sticker offering a dollar, two dollars, or even three dollars off a package. This is because all meat has a sell-by date, and if they can't sell it by then, it has to be thrown away. But don't just settle for what they already have tagged. I often want a particular cut of meat for a recipe, and if I find a package that is within a couple of days of expiring, I will bring it to the meat counter and ask them if they will discount it for me. I've never been turned down, and sometimes I've gotten real bargains that way. (And if you spot a good, discounted package you won't be using right away, you can always stick it in the freezer until the next feast comes around.)

USE FRUITS AND VEGETABLES THAT ARE IN SEASON. Food that is in season is almost always cheaper (and fresher) than food that isn't. Take asparagus, for example. When it is in season (usually about six to eight weeks during the spring), it can cost about $1.99 a pound; sometimes even less. But the rest of the year, it is often $2.99 or even $3.99 a pound. So, you will notice that the recipe for asparagus is in the Ostara section since that is when it is just starting to show up in my area. Also, as Pagans, we try to be in touch with the natural world around us, and our holidays celebrate that connection. What better way to build on that than by eating the foods that are in season in the area where you live?

BUY LOCALLY GROWN FOODS. This is the same principle as buying in-season. If the food has less far to travel (and the sellers don't have to pay for gas, refrigerated trucks, etc.), it is likely to be cheaper. It is also better for the environment *and* the local economy, so everyone wins.

CHOOSE RECIPES WITH INEXPENSIVE INGREDIENTS. Some foods are simply less expensive, no matter what time of year it is. Certain staples, such as potatoes, pasta, and rice are usually fairly cheap. If you use them as the main ingredient in your feast dish, you can probably make something that doesn't cost much (even if you add a few fancier touches). Most of the recipes in this chapter contain a majority of ingredients that are inexpensive, easy to find, and often on sale.

Feast food should be fun, tasty, and made with love. And none of that has to cost a lot of money. The recipes that follow are grouped by holiday and usually contain various foods that are associated with that particular Sabbat. But you are free to make them any time, of course. There are also a few basic recipes for "Cakes and Ale" for Full Moon rituals, just to round things out.

If you are an inexperienced cook, you will probably want to follow the recipes pretty closely, at least the first time you make them. (Don't worry—they're all quite simple.) But if you are comfortable in the kitchen, feel free to change them in any way you'd like—add an herb, substitute one kind of vegetable for another, whatever strikes your fancy—it's your feast, after all!

IMBOLC

TRES LECHES PIE $ $

Tres Leches means "three milks." This pie is particularly appropriate for Imbolc since milk is one of the main traditional foods used to celebrate this holiday. The three milks in this case are whole milk, cream, and butter—so this is not exactly a diet pie! But everyone knows that there are no calories in feast food eaten with friends.

TIME FOR PREPARATION/COOKING:
15 minutes, plus 1 hour to set

INGREDIENTS:
- 1 nine-inch pie crust (you can make it from scratch, but I usually use one from the refrigerator section of the grocery store) if you want to get really fancy, you can substitute phyllo dough (eight or nine sheet, layered with melted butter)
- ½ cup butter (margarine will not work)
- 4 tbsp cornstarch
- 1 cup whole milk
- 1 cup heavy cream
- ¾ cup sugar
- ¼ tsp salt
- ¾ tsp vanilla extract
- ¾ tsp almond extract
- 1 tsp nutmeg
- 1 tsp cinnamon

DIRECTIONS:
- Bake the pie crust.
- Beat milk and cornstarch together in a bowl, adding the cornstarch slowly to make sure it dissolves fully. Add cream and salt.
- Melt butter over medium heat, pour milk mixture slowly into butter, stirring constantly until mixture thickens (do not boil).
- Remove from heat and add extracts, pour into pie shell, and sprinkle with spices.
- Allow to set, which will probably take about an hour.

Morgana's Cheese Fondue $ $

Cheese, of course, is a variation on milk, so a cheese fondue is also very suitable for Imbolc. This dish will be slightly more expensive but a bit fancier if you use wine. (If serving to minors or if one of your guests has a problem with alcohol, it is probably safer to use apple juice.)

TIME FOR PREPARATION/COOKING:
30 minutes in crock pot

INGREDIENTS:
- 2 cups shredded cheese (a pre-packaged 3-cheese mix is nice)
- 1 cup Chablis wine or apple juice
- 2 tsp Worchester sauce
- Cut-up pieces of bread for dipping

DIRECTIONS:
- Put all ingredients except for bread in a crock pot or regular pot on the stove, heat until cheese is hot and melted. (This is quicker to do in a regular pot but easier to keep warm in a crock pot.)

- Provide forks for spearing the bread before dipping into fondue.

Jhaea's Creamy Spinach $ $

This recipe features frozen spinach, which is fairly inexpensive and easy to use. The cheese and half-and-half symbolize the milk we use to celebrate Imbolc, and spinach is one of the earliest spring vegetables. You can substitute low-fat or fat-free cream cheese and half-and-half if you want to make this healthier. It is also easy to double if you are feeding a large crowd.

TIME FOR PREPARATION/COOKING:
30 minutes

INGREDIENTS:
- ½ cup onion, diced
- 2 cloves garlic, minced
- 1 tbsp butter
- 1 tbsp flour
- 1 cup half-and-half
- 4 oz cream cheese, cubed
- ½ tsp salt
- ⅛ tsp nutmeg
- Pepper to taste
- 1 16 oz package of frozen spinach, thawed and drained
- ¼ cup shredded Parmesan cheese
- Optional: extra cheese or pine nuts for garnish

DIRECTIONS:
- In a large pan, sauté onion until tender. When almost done, add garlic.
- Stir in flour.
- Gradually add half-and-half until blended well.

- Bring to a boil over medium heat, then reduce heat slightly and cook for 2-3 minutes, until slightly thickened.
- Add cream cheese, salt, pepper, and nutmeg. Stir until cream cheese has melted.
- Add spinach and cheese, stir until heated through.
- If desired, garnish with a little more Parmesan cheese or a few pine nuts.

Deborah's Magickal Moussaka $ $ $

This is a bit more expensive because it has meat in it. You can substitute ground beef for ground lamb if you prefer, although lamb is traditional for Imbolc. It can also be made as a vegetarian dish (and cheaper) by leaving out the meat and simply adding more eggplant.

TIME FOR PREPARATION/COOKING:
30 minutes plus 20 minutes simmering

INGREDIENTS:
- 1 large eggplant (about a lb.), cut into small pieces (you can peel it if you want to, but it isn't necessary)
- 3 tbsp olive oil
- 1 medium onion, chopped
- 1 package white mushrooms (about 8 oz), chopped
- 1 lb. ground lamb
- 1 6 oz can of tomato paste
- 1 tomato, chopped (canned is okay)
- 4 tbsp fresh parsley, chopped (reserve 1 tbsp for garnish)
- 1 tbsp of Worchester sauce
- ½ cup shredded Parmesan cheese
- 2 cloves garlic, minced

- Optional: 2 tbsp sherry or red wine, a few drops of hot sauce or a sprinkle of red pepper, sour cream for garnish

DIRECTIONS:
- Cook eggplant, mushrooms, and onion in olive oil until tender.
- Add ground lamb and garlic and cook until meat is well-done.
- Add tomato, tomato paste, Worchester sauce, wine, and hot sauce if using. Simmer about 15 minutes, until flavors are well mixed.
- Add cheese and parsley and cook another 5 minutes.
- Sprinkle with additional cheese before serving or top with a dollop of sour cream.
- Sprinkle with reserved parsley and serve.

Lauren's "Grown-Up" Hot Chocolate $ $

This hot chocolate can be made more cheaply and non-alcoholic by leaving out the liquor. On the other hand, it is absolutely delicious when made the "grown-up" way! This is a recipe that will come out a little differently every time, depending on what ingredients you decide to use.

TIME FOR PREPARATION/COOKING:
10 minutes

INGREDIENTS:
- ½ gallon milk
- 4 oz semi-sweet baker's chocolate (you can also use cocoa powder, any decent cocoa mix—the type you add milk to, not water, or chocolate syrup)

- Sugar to taste (this will depend on what kind of chocolate you use—if you use cocoa mix, you probably won't need any, but cocoa powder doesn't have sugar in it, so you'll need to add some)
- 3-5 drops peppermint extract
- 1 tsp vanilla extract
- ½ cup or more Kahlua (if not using, you can double vanilla for more flavor)
- Optional: mini marshmallows

DIRECTIONS:
- Heat milk over low temperature so it doesn't boil or curdle. Add chocolate and sugar if using and stir to mix.
- Add extracts and Kahlua, and warm through.
- Top with marshmallows if desired.
- If you want it to stay warm for the duration of the feast, a crock pot works well.

OSTARA

Ellen's Devilish Eggs $

Eggs are one of the primary foods for Ostara, as they symbolize the new life and new beginnings of spring. And you can often find them on sale, which is nice, too. It is easier to make these with large or extra-large eggs, but you can make smaller portions by using smaller eggs. I have a strong preference for free-range eggs, both on the grounds of taste and the treatment of the birds. But, of course, regular eggs are much cheaper.

TIME FOR PREPARATION/COOKING:
20 minutes

Ingredients:
- 1 dozen eggs
- ½ cup mayo
- 1 tbsp Dijon mustard
- 2 tsp horseradish sauce
- 3-4 drops Tabasco sauce
- 3-4 dashes cayenne pepper
- Optional: paprika to sprinkle on top

Directions:
- Cook eggs by gently placing them in boiling water with a spoon. Boil for about 10 minutes, then immediately drain and run eggs under cold water.
- Shell the eggs (tap gently on countertop or plate and roll to release shell). Peel shell, then cut eggs in half the long way.
- Remove yolks and place in a bowl with all other ingredients except paprika, mix well. (You can do this in a blender or food processer if you want to.)
- Mound yolk mixture into egg white halves, and sprinkle with paprika if desired.

Zanna's Asparagus Delight $ $

Asparagus is one of the first vegetables of spring. It usually goes on sale around this time of year but is fairly expensive when not in season. Luckily, a pound of asparagus goes a long way when it is being shared as a side dish, and the rest of the ingredients are inexpensive. The eggs in the hollandaise are also a good choice for an Ostara dish. If you are in a hurry, or not a great hand in the kitchen, you can substitute a pre-made hollandaise mix for the homemade one, but it won't taste nearly as good! (If you have never made hollandaise sauce before, it can be kind of tricky—you might want to experiment before trying to serve this dish to others.)

TIME FOR PREPARATION/COOKING:
15 minutes

INGREDIENTS:
- 1 lb. asparagus (more or less)
- ½ cup butter
- 3 large egg yolks
- 1 tbsp plus 1 tsp lemon juice (use fresh, not bottled)
- ⅛ tsp salt
- 2 tbsp hot water
- Optional: dash of hot pepper sauce

DIRECTIONS:
- Steam asparagus until it turns bright green. Do not overcook! (This will take 10 minutes or less.)
- While the asparagus is cooking, prepare hollandaise sauce. Melt butter in heavy pan or double boiler until hot and foamy. Do not brown.
- In a small bowl, beat eggs with lemon juice, salt and pepper, and hot sauce if using.
- Slowly add melted butter to egg mixture, followed by the water.
- Return to pan and beat over very low heat until mixture is slightly thickened. Do not overheat, or mixture will curdle and separate.
- Pour over asparagus and serve immediately, or place asparagus and sauce on oven-safe dish in low-temperature oven to keep warm, eat as soon as possible.

Goat Cheese Herbed Spread $

This is an easy, fast dish to bring that looks fancier than it is. The cost will vary depending on the price and availability of both goat cheese and fresh herbs in your area. Use fresh herbs, if possible, to symbolize the greenery of spring.

Time for preparation/cooking:
5 minutes

Ingredients:
- Roll of soft goat cheese, about ½ lb. to 1 lb.
- Fresh herbs such as parsley, chives, and basil, finely chopped
- Crackers or bread to spread the cheese on

Directions:
- Mix goat cheese and herbs together, and place in a pretty bowl. Serve with crackers or bread.

"Prosperity Pie" Quiche $ $

This is another recipe that uses eggs for their Ostara connections. The "prosperity" part of the pie comes from using herbs (and spinach) that are magickally associated with prosperity, as well as spring.

Time for preparation/cooking:
1 hour (including baking)

Ingredients:
- 1 nine-inch pie crust (pre-made is fine)
- 1½ cups shredded cheese (cheddar, Swiss, or mixed)
- 1 medium onion, chopped
- 1 cup mushrooms, sliced (can be omitted if you have folks who don't like mushrooms)

- 4 eggs
- 1½ cups milk
- 3 tbsp flour
- 1 cup fresh spinach, ripped into small pieces
- ¼ tsp salt
- ¼ tsp dry mustard
- Dried or fresh dill, parsley, and basil (about ½ tsp each dried, or 2 tbsp each fresh, chopped)
- Optional: ½ cup slivered almonds

DIRECTIONS:
- Place cheese inside the pie crust.
- Sauté onions and mushrooms until tender, add spinach at the end and cook until it starts to wilt.
- Put onion mixture on top of cheese.
- Beat together the eggs, milk, flour, herbs, salt, and mustard and pour on top of the other ingredients. Top with almonds if desired.
- Bake at 375°F for 40-45 minutes. It is done when the center is solid when jiggled.

BELTANE

Easy Garden Veggie Pie $

You can make this basic pie with any fresh veggies you happen to have around at this time of year.

TIME FOR PREPARATION/COOKING:
50 minutes (about 40 cooking)

INGREDIENTS:
- 2 cups fresh broccoli, chopped
- 1 medium onion, chopped
- 1 small green or red pepper, chopped

- 1 cup shredded cheddar cheese
- 1½ cups milk
- 3 eggs
- ¾ cup instant biscuit mix
- Salt and pepper to taste

DIRECTIONS:
- Set oven for 400°F and grease a pie pan.
- Mix broccoli, onions, pepper, and cheese and place in pan.
- Mix all other ingredients together until smooth and pour over veggies.
- Cook 35-40 minutes until golden brown.

Triple Goddess Spring Celebration (Tomatoes, Basil, & Fresh Mozzarella) $ $

This is an extremely simple recipe, but the few ingredients go together so well that it is a classic. You will take it up a notch if you use a really good balsamic vinegar. If you happen to have basil in your garden and already have balsamic vinegar in your cupboard, this becomes a pretty cheap dish.

TIME FOR PREPARATION/COOKING:
5 minutes

INGREDIENTS:
- Fresh mozzarella cheese (the stuff that is packaged for making lasagna isn't really good enough for this use; try to find the smaller balls that come in a tub, usually in the deli section)
- Fresh basil (fresh from the garden or produce section)
- Fresh tomatoes (if you live where there are local ripe tomatoes at this time of year, they are the best for this dish)
- Balsamic vinegar

DIRECTIONS:
- Slice the tomatoes and layer them with the cheese and basil.
- Drizzle them all with the best balsamic vinegar you can afford and enjoy!

Spinach Salad with Apples and Fresh Herbs $

This is one of my favorite spring salads; it is simple, yet the ingredients really complement each other. Feel free to make substitutions, depending on what you have around. Spinach is a really easy vegetable to grow, and if you have some in your garden, this is a perfect way to dress it up for company.

TIME FOR PREPARATION/COOKING:
5 minutes

INGREDIENTS:
- Fresh spinach (one bag, or about a pound—I highly recommend getting organic spinach, since spinach is one of the most highly sprayed veggies and organic is readily available, often for the same price as non-organic. If you buy a bag of pre-washed spinach, it will make your life much easier!)
- Two medium apples (blood oranges are lovely in this too, if you have them available), chopped
- ½ cup walnuts (pecans also work well)
- ¼ lb. (or so) blue cheese
- Sunflower seeds
- Simple vinaigrette made from olive oil, balsamic vinegar (or the vinegar of your choice), and a squirt of Dijon or honey mustard

DIRECTIONS:
- Tear spinach into bite-sized pieces, top with apples, cheese, walnuts, and sunflower seeds. Add vinaigrette and serve.

Strawberry Paradise Cake $ $

This cake is simple to make but looks and tastes divine. I prefer to make homemade whipped cream since it is easy, cheap, and tastes amazing, but if you absolutely have to, you can substitute store-bought. The strawberries are a perfect way to celebrate the start of summer, and this is definitely a sexy dessert!

TIME FOR PREPARATION/COOKING:
10 minutes

INGREDIENTS:
- Angel food cake (store-bought is fine)
- Fresh strawberries, sliced
- Whipped cream (it is easy to make whipped cream at home—simply buy a container of heavy or whipping cream, and beat it until it turns to whipped cream, about 5 minutes, add a little bit of sugar if you want it sweeter)
- Optional: chocolate sauce for drizzling

DIRECTIONS:
- Beat the cream until it is thick.
- Slice the cake in half through the middle (so you have two layers).
- Place the bottom half of the cake on a plate, layer on strawberries and whipped cream, place the top half gently on top and cover with more whipped cream and some strawberries. If desired, drizzle with chocolate sauce.

Chocolate-Dipped Strawberries $ $

The cost of this dish depends on the availability of fresh local strawberries. At this time of year, where I live, they are reasonably cheap (and I grow them in my garden, which makes them free). You can buy a nice chocolate sauce to dip them in, or do what I do, and simply melt good-quality chocolate chips (I like Ghirardelli) and use those.

TIME FOR PREPARATION/COOKING:
10 minutes

INGREDIENTS:
- Fresh whole strawberries
- Chocolate for dipping

DIRECTIONS:
- You can either hull the strawberries or leave the green leaves on to make them prettier (and give people and handle to hold on to the strawberries with, although then they have to have someplace to put the leaves when they're done).
- If using chocolate chips, you can easily melt them in the microwave in a heat-safe bowl. But do this in very short increments since chocolate melts very fast. Start out with 30 seconds, then when they start melting, go to 15-second intervals, stirring the softened chocolate each time to see how much is melted and to keep any one spot from overheating.
- Dip each strawberry in chocolate and place it on a plate or some waxed paper until the chocolate re-hardens.

LITHA

Deborah's Summer Salad $

I make this salad all summer long, and often in the spring and into the fall. And believe it or not, I get more compliments on this dish than I do on most of my fancy gourmet cooking. Go figure. When putting together a salad, feel free to substitute other fresh veggies or herbs you happen to have on hand.

TIME FOR PREPARATION/COOKING:
5 minutes

INGREDIENTS:
- Mixed young lettuce or romaine lettuce, torn into bite-sized pieces (you can also throw in some young spinach if you happen to have any)
- Grape tomatoes
- Black olives
- Shredded Parmesan cheese
- Sunflower seeds
- Fresh herbs—I like parsley, basil, and chives but you can use any you happen to have
- Simple vinaigrette salad dressing, preferably made with olive oil and balsamic vinegar (any pre-made vinaigrette will do, however—Paul Newman makes a nice one)

DIRECTIONS:
- Toss all ingredients with a vinaigrette. If you want to make a fancier presentation, you can arrange the tomatoes and black olives around the side of the bowl and place the cheese and seeds in the middle.

Jhaea's Minty Couscous Salad $

This is a cheap and simple dish, but it is one of the most popular things we serve at summer feasts. Jhaea made it up one day from things she happened to have around, but it is easy to make substitutions based on what you have on hand at the moment. Couscous is a form of pasta that cooks very quickly.

Time for preparation/cooking:
10 minutes, plus cooling time

Ingredients:
- 1 cup couscous (you can use whole wheat if you want to make this healthier)
- 1 large tomato, chopped or ½ lb. of grape tomatoes, sliced
- 2 small cucumbers (I like the pickling ones), cut up into small pieces
- Fresh mint (if you don't have mint or don't like it, you can substitute fresh parsley, basil, or both)
- Olive oil or vinaigrette

Directions:
- Cook the couscous in an equal amount of water by bringing water to a boil, placing couscous in pot, then turning the heat off and covering the pot. It will be done in 5 minutes.
- Let couscous cool (about 10 minutes—or less if you spread it out in a wide bowl), then add tomato, cuke, and mint.
- Toss lightly with oil or vinaigrette and serve chilled.

Deborah's Pasta Salad $ $

This is another one of my most popular dishes. I make it with whole wheat pasta to make it healthier, but regular pasta is fine.

TIME FOR PREPARATION/COOKING:
5 minutes, plus cooking and cooling time for pasta

INGREDIENTS:
- Rotini pasta (one package, cooked and cooled)
- 1 large tomato, or a container of grape tomatoes, sliced
- Black olives
- ¾ cup (more or less) shredded Parmesan cheese
- ¼ cup fresh parsley, chopped
- ¼ cup fresh basil, chopped
- Sunflower seeds
- Vinaigrette (olive oil, vinegar, and a smidge of Dijon mustard, beaten together)

DIRECTIONS:
- Toss all ingredients with vinaigrette and serve.

Yin-Yang Bean Spread $

If you want to get fancy, you can put this two-part spread into a round bowl and swirl it, so the two halves form a Yin-Yang shape. (We celebrate balance as one of the themes of the Summer Solstice, so this is a particularly appropriate symbol.) Or you can just serve it up in two separate bowls. A food processor makes this easier, but you can make it without one.

TIME FOR PREPARATION/COOKING:
20 minutes

INGREDIENTS:

- 1 can refried black beans (I like Beanitos organic)
- 1 can white beans (Great Northern or any other white bean)
- ½ cup salsa
- ¼ cup lemon juice (or more to taste), divided in half
- 2 cloves of garlic, minced or put through garlic press
- ¼ cup parsley (fresh is best, if using dried, use 2 tbsp)
- ½ cup sour cream, divided in half (this can be made with light sour cream with no loss of flavor)
- Salt to taste
- Crackers, bread, or tortilla chips

DIRECTIONS:

- You are making two separate spreads. For the black spread, mix the refried black beans, the salsa, half the lemon juice, half the sour cream, half the parsley, and 1 clove of garlic. Taste before adding salt, since some canned beans already have plenty added.
- For the white spread, mash the white beans by hand or in a food processor, add the remaining lemon juice, sour cream, parsley, and the other clove of garlic. Salt if needed.
- Serve with crackers, bread, or use as a dip for tortilla chips.

Watermelon Fruit Bowl $ $

This is simple but beautiful when done well. If you have fruit growing in your garden or can get some at a farmer's market, the dish will be less expensive. (It is way easier to do this if you get a seedless watermelon.)

TIME FOR PREPARATION/COOKING:
10 minutes

INGREDIENTS:
- Large watermelon, cut in half lengthwise, and with the inside removed and cubed
- Strawberries, sliced
- Apples, sliced
- Any other fruit of your choice—oranges, pears, peaches, berries, etc.
- Optional: small amount of sweetener or orange liqueur

DIRECTIONS:
- Cut watermelon in half lengthwise, remove the insides, and chop into small pieces.
- In a bowl, mix watermelon with all other fruit, and optional ingredients if using.
- Place fruit back into watermelon halves to serve.

LAMMAS

Ellen's Beer Bread $

This is one of the simplest bread recipes there is, but it tastes remarkably good (much like sourdough bread). It is also very suitable for use as "cakes" for "Cakes and Ale." Since we celebrate grains at Lammas, using flour and beer (which contains hops) works well. Besides, did I mention how easy it is?

TIME FOR PREPARATION/COOKING:
5 minutes to mix, 50-55 minutes to bake

INGREDIENTS:
- 2⅔ cups of self-rising flour OR
- 2⅔ cups regular flour plus 4 tsp baking powder & 1⅓ tsp salt
- 12 oz beer (we like to use a dark beer for more flavor, but any kind of beer will do)

DIRECTIONS:
- Mix flour (or flour, baking powder, and salt) and beer.
- Pour into lightly greased loaf pan and bake at 375°F for 50-55 minutes.
- The bread is done when it pulls away from the sides of the pan and a toothpick comes out clean.

Bread Pudding $

This is a particularly frugal recipe since you can use old or slightly stale bread in it. Again, it is very suitable for this holiday because of the grains in the bread.

TIME FOR PREPARATION/COOKING:
50 minutes (incl. baking time)

INGREDIENTS:
- 4 cups crumbled-up bread (old is fine, any type will do—feel free to use wheat bread if you want to make this a healthier dessert)
- 3 cups milk
- 3 large eggs
- 1 tbsp lemon juice
- 3 tbsp honey or maple syrup (you can use sugar if that is all you have, but it is a little nicer with one of the others)
- 2 tbsp brown sugar
- 2½ tsp vanilla extract
- 1 tsp cinnamon
- ½ tsp nutmeg
- ½ tsp salt
- Optional: 1 cup walnuts, chopped up medium apple, and/or ½ cup raisins

DIRECTIONS:
- Put bread into a baking pan (with walnuts, apples, and raisins if using).
- Mix all other ingredients and pour on top, mixing well to coat bread.
- Bake in a 350°F oven for about 35 minutes until crusty on top.

Morgana's Tomato Pie $ $

Feel free to use a pre-made pie crust for this if you are not a pastry wiz. With any luck, tomatoes will be starting to appear in your local farmer's markets (if not in your garden)—this is absolutely delicious when made with large ripe tomatoes and fresh local basil. It's like summer on a plate.

TIME FOR PREPARATION/COOKING:
50 minutes (40 minutes baking)

INGREDIENTS:
- 1 nine-inch pie crust, baked (you don't have to bake the crust for the entire time called for, but baking it at least halfway will keep the crust from turning too mushy)
- 3 large tomatoes (Morgana skins hers first by dipping them in boiling water so the skins come off easily), cut into thick slices
- ½ cup fresh basil
- ½ cup shredded cheese (the mixed cheese blends for pizza topping work well, or cheddar is good too)
- ½ cup mayo
- Optional: thinly sliced red onion

DIRECTIONS:
- Pre-bake pie crust, as above.
- Put a layer of tomato, topped with a layer of basil and onion if desired. Repeat.
- Combine cheese and mayo and spread thickly on top.
- Bake in 350°F oven for 40 minutes, until brown and bubbly on top.

Dilled Baby Potatoes $

Another really simple, easy, and inexpensive dish that everyone loves.

TIME FOR PREPARATION/COOKING:
45 minutes or less

INGREDIENTS:
- Baby potatoes—the little red ones work best, although fingerlings are nice, too.
- Olive oil or butter
- Dill (fresh if possible, but dried works okay for this)
- Sea salt (regular salt works fine, but the larger granules of the sea salt or kosher salt are a bit nicer) to taste

DIRECTIONS:
- Either boil or roast potatoes (if you boil them, you will lose a little bit of the flavor and nutritional value, but it is faster—boil for about 20 minutes, then drain; if baking, use 450°F oven for about 35 minutes).
- Put potatoes in a bowl with other ingredients and stir to mix. Serve while still hot.

Soil Celebration Layered Bean Dip $ $

Lammas is the first of three harvest festivals, so we are celebrating the bounty we receive from Mother Earth. If you layer the ingredients in this dip together, they look like soil covered with growing things (well, sort of). If you don't want to go to the trouble of making your own guacamole, you can easily buy some pre-made.

TIME FOR PREPARATION/COOKING:
20 minutes (10 if using prepared guacamole)

INGREDIENTS:
- 1 can refried black beans
- 1 container of guacamole or 1 avocado, mashed
- Juice of half a lemon
- 1 clove garlic, mashed
- 1 jar salsa
- ¼ cup parsley, chopped
- 1 tsp Worchester sauce
- Small tomato, chopped into tiny pieces
- Salt to taste
- Tortilla chips or crackers
- Optional: sour cream

DIRECTIONS:
- If making guacamole, combine avocado, lemon juice, garlic, Worchester sauce, half the parsley, ¼ cup salsa, and half the chopped tomatoes. Salt to taste.
- In a container or bowl (preferably glass, so you can see the layers), spread the refried beans on the bottom, top with a layer of guacamole, then with salsa and the rest of the chopped tomato. If desired, spread a thin layer of sour cream.
- Sprinkle parsley on top.
- Serve with tortilla chips or crackers.

MABON

Deborah's Corn Casserole $

Corn is one of the main foods used to celebrate Mabon, the second harvest festival. Where I live, fresh corn on the cob is one of the best benefits of growing a garden or going to a local farmer's market. This recipe uses fresh corn but can also be made with frozen in a pinch.

TIME FOR PREPARATION/COOKING:
50 minutes (30 minutes cook time)

INGREDIENTS:
- 4 ears fresh corn (can substitute 1 10 oz package of frozen if necessary) with kernels cut off the ears
- Large onion, chopped
- 2 tbsp butter
- 2 tbsp flour
- 1 tsp salt
- ½ tsp paprika
- ¼ tsp dry mustard
- Pepper to taste
- ¼ cup fresh parsley, chopped (can use fresh basil if preferred)
- ¾ cup half-and-half
- 1 large egg, beaten
- ⅓ cup Italian-flavored breadcrumbs
- ⅓ cup sliced almonds
- ¼ cup olive oil or melted butter
- Optional: ½ cup shredded Parmesan cheese

DIRECTIONS:
- Sauté onions in butter until soft.
- Stir in flour, salt, pepper, paprika, and mustard and stir over low heat until it bubbles.

- Add half-and-half gradually and heat until boiling (about a minute or two).
- Turn off heat and add corn, parsley, and egg. Stir to mix, pour into a casserole dish. (If you want, you can stir in shredded cheese at this point.)
- Sprinkle breadcrumbs over top, along with the almonds and a little bit more parsley if desired. Drizzle with melted butter or olive oil, cook at 350°F for 30-35 minutes, until browning on top and bubbly.

Baked Apple Surprise $

Baked apples are a simple, inexpensive, and healthy dessert. When making this for feast food, use the smallest apples you can find so everyone can have one, or if you will be serving a large crowd, you can use large apples and people can take part of one. If possible, use apples grown in your area, since Mabon is the second harvest festival.

Time for preparation/cooking:
45 minutes (mostly cooking time), less if using a microwave instead of a conventional oven

Ingredients:
- A dozen or so apples (depending on how many people you have coming)
- ½ cup maple syrup (you can substitute brown sugar or honey if you don't have syrup, but don't use artificial syrup)
- ½ cup walnuts
- ½ cup raisins
- Cinnamon to taste
- Optional: whipping cream or canned whipped cream

DIRECTIONS:
- Cut the core of the apples out, leaving a little at the base of the apple if possible.
- Into each apple, place a few walnuts, a few raisins, a drizzle of maple syrup, and a sprinkle of cinnamon.
- Bake in 375°F oven for about 40 minutes or until apples are soft. They can also be done in the microwave, a few at a time. Times will vary, but start out with 2 minutes, and then check at 1-minute intervals.
- If desired, serve with chilled whipped cream.

Orange Baked Beets $

Beets are another good harvest food since they are starting to be plentiful and are often inexpensive. If you want to get fancy, you can buy various different colored beets (they now come in various shades of red, red with white stripes, orange, and other interesting varieties) and mix them together.

TIME FOR PREPARATION/COOKING:
1 hour 10 minutes (1 hour cooking)

INGREDIENTS:
- 8 large or 12 medium beets
- 2 oranges
- Salt and pepper to taste
- ¼ tsp cinnamon
- Optional: thinly sliced red onion

DIRECTIONS:
- Peel beets and cut into thin slices.
- Grate the zest of both oranges and squeeze out the juice.
- Slice the remains of oranges thinly.
- Layer beets, orange slices, and onions if using.

- Sprinkle with orange zest, salt, and pepper, and pour juice over.
- Cover and bake for 1 hour at 350°F.

Lemon & Thyme Potato Gratin $

Potatoes are a good symbol for this harvest holiday, and they have the added benefit of being cheap (they are also easy to grow if you happen to have a garden). Use fresh thyme for this to bring out the added flavor of the season.

TIME FOR PREPARATION/COOKING:
1 hour (50 minutes cooking time)

INGREDIENTS:
- 2 tbsp butter (plus some for the pan or a bit of oil)
- 2 lbs. potatoes, peeled and sliced as thinly as possible (Yukon Gold potatoes work very well for this)
- 2 tsp fresh thyme leaves, chopped
- ⅛ tsp nutmeg
- Zest of one lemon, finely chopped (about 2 tsp)
- 1 cup milk
- Salt and pepper to taste
- Optional: 1 tbsp fresh rosemary and/or parsley, slivered almonds

DIRECTIONS:
- Brush the bottom of a baking dish (about 8x8, although a pie pan will do as well if necessary) with melted butter or olive oil.
- Layer one-third of the potato slices, sprinkle with lemon zest, thyme, nutmeg, other herbs if using, and salt and pepper.
- Repeat two more times, then cover all with milk. If desired, top with slivered almonds and a sprinkle of herbs.

- Cover with aluminum foil and bake for 40 minutes.
- Remove foil and bake another 10-20 minutes until the potatoes are tender and the top is browned.

SAMHAIN

Colcannon $

This is a traditional Samhain dish and has the added benefit of being simple and cheap! One of Blue Moon Circle's favorites.

TIME FOR PREPARATION/COOKING:
30 minutes

INGREDIENTS:
- 4 cups mashed potatoes (I like to use red potatoes and leave the skins on, but you can use any type you want and remove the skins if you don't like them—personally, I like the added nutrition…and I'm too lazy to peel potatoes!)
- 2½ cups chopped cooked cabbage
- ½ cup butter
- ½ cup cream, half-and-half, or milk (I use cream—it's a holiday, after all)
- 1 large onion, chopped
- ⅓ cup fresh parsley or basil, chopped
- Salt and pepper to taste

DIRECTIONS:
- Sauté onions and cabbage in a bit of butter until soft.
- Mash the rest of the butter with potatoes and cream, add to veggies, and stir until warm.
- Add parsley right before serving.

Roasted Roots $

Samhain is the third and final harvest festival. Root vegetables are usually plentiful now. They also represent the harvest that earlier Pagan folks would have tucked away in their root cellars to keep them going through the winter, as well as our own withdrawal into a quieter, more restful state.

TIME FOR PREPARATION/COOKING:
1 hour

INGREDIENTS:
- 3-4 pounds mixed root vegetables: I like to use potatoes, carrots, and beets, but any root veggies will do, including rutabagas, parsnips, etc.
- 2 large onions
- 4-5 cloves of garlic
- ¼ cup olive oil
- Sea salt or kosher salt (something large-grained, although you can use regular salt if that's all you have)
- Freshly ground pepper (again, regular pepper is okay, just not as nice)
- 2 tbsp dried or fresh rosemary, parsley, or combination

DIRECTIONS:
- Cut all the vegetables into bite-sized pieces (about an inch square).
- Toss all ingredients together in a large pan (you want to have space to spread the veggies out since root vegetables cook slowly) and cook in a 375°F oven for 45-55 minutes.
- Vegetables are done when a fork slides into them easily.

Pumpkin Soup $ $

Pumpkins are a tradition for this holiday, so pumpkin soup is a natural. If you want to dress up the presentation, you can buy a bunch of little pumpkins, hollow them out, and serve the soup inside them (instead of a bowl). Very cool!

TIME FOR PREPARATION/COOKING:
30 minutes to 1 hour (depending on whether or not you are using fresh pumpkins)

INGREDIENTS:
- A dozen small pumpkins (or you can buy two large cans of pumpkin if you don't want the fuss of cleaning fresh ones)
- Oil for pan
- 1½ tbsp butter
- 1 large onion, thinly sliced
- 1 tbsp fresh ginger, grated OR ¼ tsp dried ginger
- 3 cups water (you may need to add more)
- Salt and pepper to taste
- Optional: ½ cup cream or half-and-half

DIRECTIONS:
- If you will be using small pumpkins: cut stem end off, about ¼ of the way down. Clean and set aside.
- Remove the string and seeds and set seeds aside.
- Place pumpkins upside down on an oiled baking sheet and cook for about 40 minutes in a 350°F oven. (When they're ready, the flesh will be tender and poke easily with a fork.)
- Once the pumpkins have cooled enough to handle, scoop out flesh from inside, leaving enough so pumpkins retain their shape. Set aside.

- Toss pumpkin seeds with oil, sprinkle with salt, and place on a baking sheet. Cook for about 20 minutes or until crisp. Set aside.
- Sauté onion with butter and ginger until soft. Add pumpkin flesh and water, and simmer for about 20 minutes.
- Using a blender or food processor, puree pumpkin mixture (you will probably have to do this in a couple of batches). If desired, add more water or cream until the soup is the thickness you like.
- Return to stove to reheat. While soup is re-heating, place empty pumpkin shells (if using) on a cookie sheet, and warm in oven for about 10 minutes.
- Fill with soup and sprinkle with reserved pumpkin seeds, if desired.

Deborah's Squash Delight $

Squash is another seasonal food, as are apples.

TIME FOR PREPARATION/COOKING:
30 minutes

INGREDIENTS:
- 1 butternut squash, cut up into small pieces
- 1 large apple, chopped
- 1 large red onion, chopped
- ¾ cup walnuts
- ¾ cup dried cranberries
- 1 tbsp olive oil
- ½ cup apple cider
- Salt, pepper, and cinnamon to taste
- Optional: 1 tbsp butter, rice or pasta

DIRECTIONS:
- Sauté squash and onion in olive oil until almost soft.
- Add apple, walnuts, cranberries, and butter (if using) and cook for about 5 more minutes until the fruit softens.
- Add spices and apple cider, cook a few more minutes until squash is completely soft. If desired, serve over rice or pasta.

Samhain Devil's Food Cake $

You can, of course, make a Devil's food cake from scratch for this recipe, if you are a good cook and have the time. For most of us, a cake mix will work just fine (I won't tell if you won't).

TIME FOR PREPARATION/COOKING:
1 hour (to make cake and then decorate)

INGREDIENTS:
- Devil's food cake mix, prepared as directed. For the fanciest presentation, use a Bundt cake pan, but any size or shape of pan will do.
- Chocolate or white frosting (again, you can make it from scratch, but there are some pretty good, relatively inexpensive ones available)
- Candy decorations—some of my favorites are "red hot" cinnamon candies, the little candy corns and candy corn pumpkins, or other orange candies

DIRECTIONS:
- Bake the Devil's food cake as directed.
- Let cool, then cover with either chocolate or white frosting (depending on how devilish you are feeling).

- Decorate with holiday candy, such as those listed above. (Kids are especially entertained by this cake, although "big kids" like it, too.)

YULE

Wassail $ $

Wassail is a traditional Yule drink (remember the Christmas song about "here we come a-wassailing"?) that is essentially spiced apple cider with some form of alcohol in it. In fact, Yule used to be a pretty rowdy holiday, since folks would go wassailing from house to house…to house. That's a lot of spiked cider! You can make this as strong or weak as desired. If serving a mixed crowd of adults and children, you can make an alcoholic version for the adults and a non-alcoholic version for the kids and non-drinkers. It is especially easy if you make this in a crock pot and will stay warm for the duration of your celebration.

TIME FOR PREPARATION/COOKING:
20 minutes (including heating time)

INGREDIENTS:
- 1 gallon apple cider
- 1-2 cups either red wine, whiskey, or brandy
- Spice mixture, including some or all of the following: allspice, cloves, cinnamon, and ginger. (You can use whole spices and float them in a tea ball or mesh bag or toss in a few cinnamon sticks. If you use dried and powdered spices, you will want to use a bit less.)
- ½ cup of maple syrup or honey (you might need less, depending on the sweetness of the cider

and which form of alcohol you are using—start with a small amount and add more to taste)
- Optional: apples sliced across to make a pentacle shape or orange slices (for decoration)

DIRECTIONS:
- Place all ingredients in a pot or crock pot. Adjust spices and sweetener to taste.
- Float apple or orange slices on top if desired.
- Heat until warmed through. And shout "Wassail" which means, "To your health!"

Holly & Mistletoe Veggies $ $

Holly and mistletoe are the origins of the green and red theme of this holiday, and Christmas as well. You can substitute any other green or red veggies in this simple dish.

TIME FOR PREPARATION/COOKING:
40 minutes

INGREDIENTS:
- 1 head of broccoli, chopped into bite-sized pieces
- Package of frozen peas
- 2 red peppers, chopped
- Medium red onion, chopped
- ½ tsp garlic powder or 1 clove garlic, minced
- 1 tbsp dried dill or 2 tbsp fresh dill, chopped
- 1 tbsp dried parsley or 2 tbsp fresh parsley, chopped
- ¼ cup olive oil
- ⅛ cup vinegar
- Few sprinkles soy sauce

DIRECTIONS:
- Put all ingredients into a casserole dish, mix well.
- Bake at 350°F for about 30 minutes.

Orange Duckling $ $ $

This is a more expensive recipe, but if you have a formal dinner party for Yule, as Blue Moon Circle does, it is nice to have a fancy centerpiece for the meal. Duck is not as expensive as you'd think, and not much more difficult to cook than a roasted chicken. Just be aware that duck is very fatty (that's what makes it taste so good!) and can make a mess of your oven.

TIME FOR PREPARATION/COOKING:
3 hours

INGREDIENTS:
- 1 duckling (about 4 pounds)
- Small onion, finely minced
- 2 cloves garlic, finely minced
- 2 tbsp butter
- ½ cup orange juice (or juice from 1 orange)
- 2 tbsp or more orange zest (from 1 orange)
- ⅛ tsp dried mustard
- 1 tbsp dried rosemary
- 1 tbsp dried parsley
- ⅛ tsp salt
- 2 tsp cornstarch
- Optional: whole orange, sliced into rings for decoration

DIRECTIONS:
- Prepare duckling by patting dry, tucking wing tips under the back, and trimming neck skin if desired. Place breast-side up on a rack in a shallow roasting pan.
- Sauté onion and garlic in butter until soft, add other ingredients except for cornstarch, and cook until well blended, about 5-10 minutes.

- Take half of orange mixture and use it to glaze the duckling. If desired, decorate top of duckling with orange rings.
- Cook ducking in 325°F oven for 2½ to 3 hours, until meat reaches 185°F on a meat thermometer or juices run clear. You may want to occasionally use a turkey baster to remove some of the fat from the bottom of the pan.
- When done, remove from oven and let rest for 15-20 minutes.
- While duck is resting, mix the other half of orange mixture with cornstarch, and heat on stove at medium temperature until mixture thickens and boils. Pour over duck just before serving.

Rum Cake $ $

This is one of my favorite "special occasion" desserts. It takes a little more work than a regular cake, but the results are worth it! If you want to get really extravagant, you can substitute a chocolate cake mix for the yellow one, and raspberry liqueur (such as Chambord) or orange liqueur (such as Grand Marnier) for the rum. They are both pretty pricy, though. This cake is intended to be made in a Bundt pan, although you could probably use a regular pan if you had to. (I've never tried it.)

TIME FOR PREPARATION/COOKING:
1 hour 10 minutes (50-60 minutes baking time)

INGREDIENTS:
- 1 box cake mix with pudding in it (yellow or chocolate)
- 3 eggs
- ⅓ cup cooking oil
- ½ cup pecans or sliced almonds

- ½ cup rum plus ⅓ cup rum (½ cup is for cake, ⅓ cup is for glaze)
- ½ cup butter (1 stick)
- 1 cup sugar
- ½ cup water plus ¼ cup water (cake/glaze)
- Oil and flour to grease pan

DIRECTIONS:
- Grease and flour a Bundt pan.
- Mix the cake mix, eggs, ½ cup rum, ½ cup water, and ⅓ cup oil.
- Put nuts on the bottom of the pan, then pour cake mixture over them. Bake at 325°F for 50-60 minutes until a toothpick comes out clean.
- For glaze, in a pan on the stove, mix sugar, ½ cup butter, ⅓ cup rum, and ¼ water.
- Boil for 2-3 minutes, then pour over cake. Let sit for a while so cake can absorb glaze.

FULL MOON CAKES & ALE

CAKES

Ellen's Ginger Moon Cookies $

These are Blue Moon Circle's favorites!

TIME FOR PREPARATION/COOKING:
10 minutes prep, 2 hours chill time, 12 minutes baking time

INGREDIENTS:
- 1 box spice cake mix
- 1 cup flour
- 2 tsp ginger
- 2 eggs

- ⅓ cup oil
- ½ cup molasses

DIRECTIONS:
- Mix dry ingredients together. Add wet ingredients and mix well. (Note that this makes a stiff, hard dough. It can be difficult to use a mixer on it, so you will probably have to mix it by hand.)
- Cover and chill for 2 hours. Shape into Full Moon or Half Moon shapes and bake on a greased cookie sheet for 12-15 minutes (depending on size of cookies) at 375°F.
- You can also stamp these cookies with interesting designs. Ellen usually presses them with a pentacle stamp.

Marvelous Monkey Bread $

This recipe is so simple, yet so yummy. The trick is to use store-bought frozen bread dough (although you can certainly make your own if you want to go to the trouble).

TIME FOR PREPARATION/COOKING:
10 minutes prep plus 40 minutes bake time

INGREDIENTS:
- Loaf frozen bread dough, thawed and allowed to rise
- 1 stick butter, melted
- ½ cup sugar
- 2 tbsp cinnamon
- Optional: walnuts or pecans, chopped

DIRECTIONS:
- Thaw the bread dough and allow to rise, then roll into small balls about an inch or two around.

- Roll balls of dough into melted butter, then roll in mixture of cinnamon and sugar. Place in Bundt pan.
- Layer the next bunch of balls on top of the first. Mix in nuts as you go if desired.
- Drizzle any remaining butter on top.
- Bake in a 350°F oven for 40 minutes or until browning on top.

Jhaea's Lemon-Lavender Cookies $

When Blue Mooner Jhaea got married (I officiated at the wedding, which was a wonderful affair), she gave each guest a little card with this recipe and the one for the rosemary shortbread cookies below, attached with a ribbon to another card with an explanation for the wedding wishes associated with those herbs. It was one of the most popular wedding favors I have ever seen.

TIME FOR PREPARATION/COOKING:
20 minutes

INGREDIENTS:
- 1 cup butter (2 sticks)
- ½ cup brown sugar
- 1 cup sugar
- 2 eggs
- ⅓ cup sour cream
- 2 tbsp lemon juice
- 1 tbsp grated lemon zest
- 4 cups flour
- 1 tbsp baking powder
- 1 tbsp baking soda
- 2 tbsp lavender flowers
- Optional: ½ cup sliced almonds

DIRECTIONS:
- Cream butter and sugars, add eggs, sour cream, zest, and vanilla, and beat well.
- In a separate bowl, mix flour, baking powder, baking soda, and lavender. Add to creamed mixture and mix.
- Put a teaspoon of mixture for each cookie onto greased cookie sheet and bake at 350°F for about 10 minutes.

Rosemary Shortbread Cookies $

These make an especially nice and simple cookie for "cakes." You can serve them at the Samhain ritual since rosemary is for remembrance.

TIME FOR PREPARATION/COOKING:
1 hour (50 minutes baking time)

INGREDIENTS:
- 1 cup butter
- 1 cup sugar
- 3 cups flour
- 3 tbsp rosemary, finely chopped

DIRECTIONS:
- Cream together butter and sugar. Add 2½ cups of the flour and the rosemary.
- Knead dough on surface dusted with the other ½ cup of flour until the dough cracks.
- Roll into ¼ inch thick layer and cut into shapes (Half Moon cookie cutters are great for this, although a round cutter will make a Full Moon shape).
- Bake on ungreased cookie sheet for about 50 minutes until lightly browned.

Pecan Mini-Muffins $

This is a simple way to make cakes for a crowd. You can use paper muffin liners if you want but be careful to wipe away any spatters so they don't stick.)

TIME FOR PREPARATION/COOKING:
25 minutes

INGREDIENTS:
- 1 cup brown sugar
- ½ cup flour
- 1 cup pecans, chopped
- ⅔ cup butter, melted and cooled
- 2 eggs, beaten

DIRECTIONS:
- Mix sugar, flour, and pecans.
- In a separate bowl, mix butter and eggs, and combine all ingredients.
- Pour into greased and floured mini-muffin tins (⅔ full) and bake at 350°F for 18-20 minutes. Muffins are done when a toothpick comes out clean.
- Cool on racks.

ALE

Pomegranate Passion $ $

I like to use pomegranate juice for "ale" because of its association with the goddess Persephone and for its sweet and slightly exotic taste. It isn't, however, the cheapest juice out there. You can always substitute grape juice if you want to spend a little less, or whatever juice you can find on sale (cranberry works well).

TIME FOR PREPARATION/COOKING:
5 minutes

INGREDIENTS:
- Pomegranate juice
- Seltzer or club soda
- ½ lemon

DIRECTIONS:
- In a pitcher or chalice, mix pomegranate juice with sparkling water (about ⅔ juice to ⅓ soda), add a squeeze of lemon. If desired, float a slice of lemon on top.

Spiced Cider $

This is particularly nice for "Cakes and Ale" for the fall Full Moons and the three harvest Sabbats.

TIME FOR PREPARATION/COOKING:
10 minutes

INGREDIENTS:
- Jug of apple cider
- ¼ tsp cinnamon
- ⅛ tsp nutmeg
- 1 tbsp dried or fresh lemon rind or zest
- Optional: a few cloves

DIRECTIONS:
- You can serve this cold, but it is even nicer if you warm it up. Combine all ingredients.
- If serving cold, let sit for at least half an hour. If serving warm, place in a pot and simmer for about 10 minutes.

Herbed Ice Cubes for Water or Wine $

If you want to add a witchy touch to a simple chalice of water or wine, you can make ice cubes ahead of time that have herbs associated with whatever magick you are working that night.

TIME FOR PREPARATION/COOKING:
2 hours, or however long it takes your freezer to make ice

INGREDIENTS:
- Water
- Herbs: lemon balm and mint work particularly well for this, although you can also use rose petals, basil, or any other edible herb.

DIRECTIONS:
- Fill an ice cube tray with water, sprinkle herbs into each compartment, and freeze. Later, you can add them to the chalice of wine or water, or most other "ales."

CHAPTER 7

FIFTY WAYS TO PRACTICE WITCHCRAFT FOR LITTLE OR NO MONEY

We've talked a lot in this book about ways to save money in your practice of the Craft. But the truth is, there are many ways to walk the Pagan path without spending any money at all. Here are fifty simple suggestions to get you started.

Most of these are probably activities you do already or could easily add to your life. What makes them into a Witchcraft practice is your intent and focus when you do them.

If you maintain a mindful awareness of your connection to the environment around you (and to the gods) as you follow these suggestions, they move from the realm of the mundane into the magickal.

If you can, try and do at least one of these every day.

TAKE A WALK IN THE WOODS.
Use all your senses and try to spot plants or animals you might usually miss. Find something small (like an acorn, a leaf, or a rock, for instance) and bring it home to put on your altar.

SIT BY A BODY OF WATER.
It doesn't matter if it is an ocean, a lake, a river, or the tiniest stream. Listen to the sounds the water makes and feel them soothe your soul.

WALK OUTSIDE AT NIGHT AND GAZE AT THE STARS.
Feel how small you are, and yet, how much you are a part of the universe around you.

WALK OUTSIDE AT NIGHT AND LOOK AT THE MOON.
What phase is it in? How might that phase correspond to something that is happening in your life?

TALK TO THE GODDESS OR GOD OF YOUR CHOICE.
You can do this standing at your altar, under the Full Moon, or while sitting in a quiet corner of nature. You don't have to say anything profound or even ask a question. Just say, "Hi, I know you're there."

KISS SOMEONE YOU LOVE.
Channel the love of the gods into the kiss you give and feel it coming back to you in the kiss you receive in return.

PUT YOUR HANDS IN THE DIRT.
Gardening is an easy way to get in touch with our Pagan natures, but if you can't have a garden, try planting a few little herbs inside or a flowering plant or two.

WALK IN THE RAIN.
As you get wet, feel the water in the droplets connecting you to the biggest ocean and continents far away.

PET AN ANIMAL.
Animals connect us to the wild side of life (no matter how tame they may appear). If you don't have a pet of your own, try going to a zoo (or a friend's house).

Sing or chant.

Praise the Goddess with your voice without worrying about how you sound.

Beat on a drum.

Feel the rhythm of your heart, feel the slap of your hands on the drumhead, and be connected to all the Pagans who have ever drummed.

Light a candle.

It doesn't have to be a magickal candle, and you don't have to be casting a spell. Simply add a little light to the world for a moment or two and enjoy the flickering flame. If you want to, test your magickal abilities by seeing if you can make the flame rise a little, just by concentrating on making it happen.

Say "Thank you."

We ask the gods for many things over the course of time—it is a good idea to take a few minutes every day and list the people, places, and events in our lives that we are grateful for. These don't have to be big things. Just whatever made your day a little better.

Meditate on peace.

We know how powerful words and thoughts are. If we each took a moment every day to close our eyes (even if just for two or three minutes) and meditate on a world full of peace, who knows what we might achieve?

Smile at someone for no particular reason.

Smiles are contagious. Try smiling at someone and see if they don't smile back. Bring a little more joy into someone's day.

Look at everyone as though they
were beautiful.
The Goddess loves us all and thinks we are all beautiful. If
you try, you can see others with a glimmer of how She sees
them. Try it; you will be amazed.

Help someone out.
The gods help those who help themselves. But sometimes
we do the gods' work for them as a part of walking our talk.
Don't help because you have to or because you might get
something in return—help because it is a way to channel a
little bit of the divine through yourself.

Take a bath.
Put some magickal or medicinal (or both) herbs in the
water and add a little sea salt. Light a candle in the room,
if it is safe to do so, and you will have all four elements.
And a few moments of relaxing peace and quiet to soak
away the day's cares and reconnect with your own inner
peace. Scrub your skin with a handful of sea salt and feel
the connection with a distant shore.

Take a look into the future or try to get
some clarity about the past or the present.
If you already have a tarot deck or some rune stones, you
can use them. But you can also gaze into a bowl of water,
try your hand at reading tea leaves, or simply ask a question
and listen for the answer.

Make love.
Sex with someone you love is not only fun and enjoyable,
but also a way of connecting with the energy of the God
and/or Goddess. Be mindful of this connection during the
act and see if that changes the experience for you.

PLANT A TREE.

Anything that we do to help replenish Mother Gaia is an act of grace and worship. Planting a tree doesn't have to cost more than a dollar or two, and it will be a gesture that lasts for many years. Just think—you will have helped the planet to make more air.

CLEAN UP A ROADSIDE OR A BEACH.

Take a walk down any road or on most beaches and you will probably see evidence of human beings and their debris. Take a plastic bag with you, and as you enjoy your walk, pick up any garbage you find along the way. Your Mother will thank you.

RECYCLE.

Anything we do that lessens our negative impact on the Earth is a good thing, and recycling can become a part of walking your talk. It costs nothing and helps the Earth. In places with can and bottle deposits, it can even get you a little bit of money.

PLAY WITH A CHILD.

Children are our future (and some of them are even future Pagans). Anything we do to nurture and support a child is also an act of grace. And if you're doing it right, it can even be fun. If you don't have kids of your own, offer to play with a friend's child for an hour—they'll love you for it!

VOLUNTEER.

The act of giving unselfishly to others takes a little time, but no money. And the returns can be amazing. Try visiting a nursing home and reading to a resident who rarely gets visitors. Or help start a collection of canned food for a local food pantry. Volunteering is a way of opening your heart to others; it doesn't have to be anything huge or time-consuming. But you might find it addictive, in its own way.

PRAY.
Prayer is a form of communication with the gods. It doesn't have to be formal or take place at an altar. Simply close your eyes and speak from the heart. Sometimes you may ask for help with some specific issue, or an answer to a question that has been troubling you. Sometimes you may just ask for protection for yourself and those you love. There is no right or wrong way to pray. You just do it.

LAUGH.
The gods love the sound of laughter.

DANCE FOR JOY.
Put on some music that makes your feet want to move and dance for the delight of dancing. Make your dance into an expression of joy, and revel in your body's ability to move.

LEARN SOMETHING.
Part of our task here on Earth is to become our own best selves. One of the ways to make ourselves better is to increase our knowledge of the world around us. You can learn about an aspect of nature, a spiritual path, or anything else that catches your interest. Simply make an effort to learn something new now and then. It's good for your brain to make it work a little harder on occasion.

SEND GOOD ENERGY TO SOMEONE WHO NEEDS IT.
Our energy and positive thoughts are powerful things— share them with someone who needs a little boost.

LEARN A FORM OF HEALING.
This can be something like massage, reiki, reflexology, or any other healing modality that taps into your own energy and your two strong hands. And you don't have to take expensive classes to learn most of this stuff, either. Find a book or someone you know who already has a

healing skill and is willing to teach you. Anyone can learn to heal; you just have to try. And then you can use those healing abilities to make other folks feel better. (And you can use most of them on yourself, too.)

PHONE A MEMBER OF YOUR FAMILY OR A CLOSE FRIEND.

We spend a lot of time rushing around, trying to keep up with our hectic lives. Sometimes that means we don't reach out to the people we love quite as often as we mean to. Take a few minutes out of your busy day to stop and phone someone close to you; check in on their lives, say hello, and let them know you are thinking of them.

SURPRISE SOMEONE WITH A SMALL GIFT FOR NO PARTICULAR REASON.

This doesn't have to be something expensive—a flower, a beautiful leaf, or a fresh-baked cookie will do.

TAKE OFF YOUR SHOES AND FEEL THE EARTH.

Focus on the way the dirt (or sand) feels and connect your energy to the planet beneath you. Send down roots and draw up the energy of the planet.

FLY A KITE AND CONNECT WITH THE AIR.

Feel the wind pull on your kite and acknowledge the power of the element.

EXPLORE YOUR SENSES.

Go outside and listen. Do you hear birds, or the wind, or the sound of children's laughter? What can you smell? Is it pleasant or unpleasant, natural or man-made? Notice the little things you might normally ignore; see the tiny insects moving in the earth, or the trails from an airplane overhead.

LISTEN TO YOUR INNER VOICE.
Many times, when we have questions, we already know the answers. We simply don't listen to our own inner wisdom. If you need an answer, take some time to close your eyes and listen to that small, quiet voice that resides within each of us. Have faith in your own wisdom.

RECONNECT WITH YOUR INNER CHILD.
Eat an ice cream cone, twirl a hula hoop, turn cartwheels, swing on a swing—do something that reconnects you with your own inner child and lets you remember the joys of being young at heart, no matter what your age.

NAP.
Regenerate your energy.

BE KIND TO YOURSELF.
Instead of being self-critical, tell yourself you are doing a good job. Reward yourself for your accomplishments. Say nice things to yourself without being self-conscious about it.

EXPLORE SOMEONE ELSE'S VIEWPOINT.
We want people to accept us and our particular form of spiritual belief. In return, it is good to make an effort to see what other people believe and how they worship.

STAND UNDER THE LIGHT OF THE FULL MOON.
Feel the lunar energy infuse your soul.

LISTEN TO THE RAIN.
Open a window and listen to the rain pouring down outside or pay attention to the sound it makes on your roof or windows. Rain comes from the heavens and is a form of natural music—stop and listen to it play.

GET UP EARLY AND WATCH THE SUN COME UP.
Think of the possibilities in a new day.

WRITE IN A JOURNAL.
Keep track of your thoughts and look out for patterns that don't work for you. Write down both good things and bad and see if there is balance in your life or if you have a tendency to swing toward the negative. See what changes and what doesn't and figure out what that means for your future.

PAY ATTENTION TO YOUR DREAMS.
Dreams can have many messages for us. Try to remember what you dreamed about, and maybe even write down the ones that seem important. You may be getting a message from your own inner wisdom or from some outside source. Pay attention to those dreams that reoccur or seem to carry special weight.

FOCUS ON WHAT YOU'RE EATING.
Be mindful of where it came from and give thanks to those who worked to produce it and get it to your table. Savor the tastes and textures. Be grateful to have food to eat at all when many people don't. Enjoy it, instead of simply using it to fuel your body.

WISH UPON A STAR.

MAKE TIME TO SPEND WITH THE PEOPLE YOU LOVE.
Life is short, and no one ever said at the end, "I wish I'd spent more time at work." No matter how busy you are, make sure you take the time to be with the people who are important to you. All acts of love are acts of worship—and that can include something as small as having dinner with your family.

GIVE YOURSELF A HUG.
Put your arms around yourself and channel the love of the Goddess. Feel her hugging you as you hug yourself and feel her love surrounding you.

CHAPTER 8

THE EVERYDAY WITCH—
WHEN BEING A WITCH DOESN'T
MEAN BUYING MORE STUFF

We've talked about inexpensive tools and cheap ways to feed yourself and all your witchy friends. We've talked about Crafty crafts and simple ways to practice that don't cost you much—if anything. We've talked about how to find supplies and information, and all the other ways there are to walk the path without spending money. Now I'm going to say something you might find a little shocking.

None of this really matters.

Gulp.

Now, I'm not saying that this book, and all the suggestions it contains, isn't useful. I certainly hope it is. I sincerely believe that it will help you to practice your Craft while spending less money, and that is definitely a good thing.

But it isn't the most important thing.

The truth is the practice of Witchcraft isn't about *stuff*. It isn't about crafts, or feast foods, or tools, or even books. (Okay, maybe it's a little about books.)

To me, at least, being a Witch is about *connection*. It is about that feeling you get when you stand under the Full Moon and feel the solid, tangible presence of the Goddess.

It is about the goosebumps that rise on your arms during a really good ritual when you cast the circle hand to hand and feel the spark of connection pass from person to person. Or when you cast a spell standing alone in front of your altar and feel that shiver in the air that means that *something* has changed in the world because of you.

Witchcraft is acknowledging the power and magnificence of nature and our connection to the universe around us, from the smallest butterfly to the immense solar system in which we live. It is standing in the midst of a forest and feeling both insignificant and part of something huge and wonderful, all at the same time.

Witchcraft is sensing that which you shouldn't be able to sense, glimpsing the past and the future, and knowing that there are levels of existence beyond the obvious, mundane world. Witchcraft is intuition on overdrive, faith in the face of overwhelming reality, and applying the force of your will to change that reality into something better.

Tools are handy, useful, and fun. Books can expand your knowledge and further your practice. And feasts, well, feasts are a way to gather together and celebrate the bounty and the joy and the community that brings us together.

But they are still just forms of connection. Tools help us make the connection to our power more easily, but that power must exist already, or the tools are useless. Books help us connect to other people's knowledge and wisdom, but we have to be looking already, or we wouldn't find the books we need. Feasts are a way of connecting with each other, but we must be willing to reach out to others, or there would be no one at the table.

We are the connection. We are the power. We are the magick.

And that's what's really important.

No matter what your budget or how you decide to spend your money, there are no limitations on how well you can practice Witchcraft besides the ones you put on yourself.

You can be a powerful, talented, wise, and warm Witch without spending a penny. And you should never feel that a lack of money is an excuse for being anything less.

This book, like so many others, is a tool for you to use to make your practice, and by extension, your entire life, better. More productive. More interesting. More fun. More fulfilling.

I hope that at least some of the suggestions here will help you to achieve the Witchcraft practice you desire, without placing a strain on your budget. If that's true, then I've done my job.

The rest, my friend, is up to you.

BIBLIOGRAPHY

"13 Moons—Shop for Pagan, Metaphysical & Spiritual Supplies." *13 Moons*, http://13moons.com.

Adler, Margot. *Drawing Down the Moon*. Penguin Books, 2006.

Ardinger, Barbara. *Pagan Every Day*. Weiser Books, 2006.

Bacon, Sir Francis. *Sacred Meditations*. Simon and Schuster, 2015.

Barrette, Elizabeth. *Composing Magic*. Red Wheel/Weiser, 2007.

"BBI Media." *BBI Media - Goddess, Pagan, Wiccan and Gaian Magazines*, https://bbimedia.com/.

Blake, Deborah. *Circle, Coven & Grove: A Year of Magickal Practice*. Crossed Crow Books, 2023.

—. *Everyday Witch A to Z: An Amusing, Inspiring & Informative Guide to the Wonderful World of Witchcraft*. Llewellyn Worldwide, 2012.

—. *Everyday Witch A to Z Spellbook*. Llewellyn Worldwide, 2010.

—. *The Goddess Is in the Details*. Llewellyn Worldwide, 2009.

Bolen, Jean Shinoda. *Goddesses in Older Women*. Harper Paperbacks, 2014.

Bonewits, Isaac. *Real Magic*. Red Wheel/Weiser, 1989.

"BookMooch: Trade Your Books with Other People." *BookMooch*, http://BookMooch.com.

Buckland, Raymond. *Buckland's Complete Book of Witchcraft*. Llewellyn Worldwide, 2002.

—. *Wicca for Life: The Way of the Craft*. Citadel Press, 2018.

Chase, Pamela, and Jonathan Pawlik. *Healing with Gemstones*. New Page Books, 2002.

Cole, Jennifer. *Ceremonies of the Seasons*. Duncan Baird Publishers, 2007.

Connor, Kerri. *The Pocket Spell Creator*. New Page Books, 2003.

Cunningham, Scott. *Cunningham's Encyclopedia of Crystal, Gem & Metal Magic*. Llewellyn Worldwide, 2011.

—. *Cunningham's Encyclopedia of Magical Herbs*. Llewellyn Worldwide, 2012.

—. *Earth, Air, Fire & Water*. Llewellyn Worldwide, 2012.

—. *Living Wicca*. Llewellyn Worldwide, 2012.

—. *Magical Herbalism*. Llewellyn Worldwide, 1986.

—. *The Complete Book of Incense, Oils & Brews*. Llewellyn Worldwide, 2002.

—. *Wicca: A Guide for the Solitary Practitioner*. Llewellyn Worldwide, 2010.

Curott, Phyllis. *Book of Shadows*. Harmony Books, 1999.

De Angeles, Ly. *Witchcraft Theory and Practice*. Llewellyn Worldwide, 2012.

Digitalis, Raven. *Shadow Magick Compendium*. Crossed Crow Books, 2022.

Dubats, Sally. *Natural Magick*. Citadel Press, 2002.

Dugan, Ellen. *Cottage Witchery*. Llewellyn Worldwide, 2012.

—. *Garden Witchery*. Llewellyn Worldwide, 2013.

—. *The Enchanted Cat*. Llewellyn Worldwide, 2012.

Dumars, Denise. *Be Blessed: Daily Devotions for Busy Wiccans and Pagans*. New Page Books, 2006.

Dunwich, Gerina. *The Pagan Book of Halloween*. Penguin Compass, 2000.

—. *The Wicca Garden*. Citadel Press, 2018.

Eilers, Dana D. *The Practical Pagan*. New Page Books, 2002.

"Facing North." *Facing North*, http://Facingnorth.net.

"Famous Paintings: Wall Art Reproductions." *Overstock Art*, http://overstockArt.com.

"Fire Mountain Gems and Beads." *Wholesale Beads and Jewelry Making Supplies Fire Mountain Gems and Beads*, http://firemountaingems.com.

Fitch, Ed. *Magical Rites from the Crystal Well*. Llewellyn Worldwide, 1984.

Galenorn, Yasmine. *Embracing the Moon*. Nightqueen Enterprises LLC, 2015.

"Goddess Isis Books & Gifts - Tools for Your Soul's Journey: A Spiritual, Mystical, Metaphysical, Tarot and Wicca Superstore." *Goddess Isis Books & Gifts,* http://Isisbooks.com.

Green, Marian. *A Witch Alone: The Essential Guide for the Solo Practitioner of the Magical Arts*. Hampton Roads Publishing, 2009.

Greer, John Michael. *The New Encyclopedia of the Occult*. Llewellyn Worldwide, 2003.

Greer, Mary K. *Tarot for Your Self*. Weiser Books, 2019.

Grimassi, Raven. *Encyclopedia of Wicca & Witchcraft*. Llewellyn Worldwide, 2000.

—. *Spirit of the Witch*. Llewellyn Worldwide, 2003.

Guiley, Rosemary Ellen. *The Encyclopedia of Magic and Alchemy*. Facts on File, 2006.

—. *The Encyclopedia of Witches and Witchcraft*. Checkmark Books, 1999.

Hardie, Titania. *Titania's Magical Compendium*. Thunder Bay Press, 2003.

Henes, Donna. *The Queen of My Self*. Monarch Press, 2005.

Holland, Eileen. *Holland's Grimoire of Magickal Correspondence*. Red Wheel/Weiser, 2005.

—. *The Wicca Handbook*. Weiser Books, 2008.

Illes, Judika. *The Element Encyclopedia of Witchcraft: The Complete A–Z for the Entire Magical World*. Harper Element, 2014.

Johnstone, Michael. *The Ultimate Encyclopedia of Spells*. Gramercy Books, 2004.

Jordan, Michael. *Encyclopedia of Gods*. Echo Point Books & Media, LLC, 2022.

Kynes, Sandra. *Witches' Sabbats & Esbats*. Crossed Crow Books, 2023.

McColman, Carl. *The Well-Read Witch*. New Page Books, 2002.

McCoy, Edain. *Spellworking for Covens*. Llewellyn Worldwide, 2002.

—. *The Witch's Coven: Finding or Forming Your Own Circle*. Llewellyn Worldwide, 1997.

Morrison, Dorothy. *Bud, Blossom & Leaf*. Llewellyn Worldwide, 2001.

—. *Everyday Moon Magic*. Llewellyn Worldwide, 2012.

Moura, Ann. *Green Witchcraft*. Llewellyn Worldwide, 2014.

Nahmad, Claire. *Catspells: A Collection of Enchantments for You and Your Feline Companion*. Running Press, 1993.

"PaperBack Swap: Trade Used Books with PaperBack Swap" *PaperBack Swap*, http://paperbackswap.com.

"Pagan Path – The Original Online Academy." *Pagan Path*, http://paganpath.com.

Penczak, Christopher. *The Mystic Foundation*. Llewellyn Worldwide, 2006.

RavenWolf, Silver. *Halloween*. Llewellyn Worldwide, 1999.

Renee, Janina. *By Candlelight*. Llewellyn Worldwide, 2004.

Rosean, Lexa. *The Encyclopedia of Magickal Ingredients*. Paraview Pocket Books, 2005.

Roth, Harold. *The Witching Herbs: 13 Essential Plants and Herbs for Your Magical Garden*. Weiser Books, 2017.

Seville, Christine. *Practical Wicca the Easy Way*. Sterling Publishing Company Incorporated, 2003.

Singer, Marian. *A Witch's 10 Commandments*. Simon and Schuster, 2006.

Starhawk. *The Spiral Dance*. Harper Collins, 1999.

Sylvan, Dianne. *The Circle Within*. Llewellyn Worldwide, 2012.

Telesco, Patricia. *Advanced Wicca*. Citadel Press, 2000.

—. *Cakes And Ale for The Pagan Soul*. Crossing Press, 2005.

——. *Your Book of Shadows: How to Write Your Own Magickal Spells*. Citadel Press, 1999.

"The Blessed Bee: Your Premier Witchcraft Supply Store." *The Blessed Bee*, http://Theblessedbee.com.

Trobe, Kala. *The Witch's Guide to Life*. Llewellyn Worldwide, 2003.

Tuitean, Paul, and Estelle Daniels. *Pocket Guide to Wicca*. The Crossing Press, 1998.

Waite, Arthur Edward. *The Pictorial Key to the Tarot*. U.S. Games Systems, 1997.

Weinstein, Marion. *Earth Magic*. New Page Books, 2003.

——. *Positive Magic*. Weiser Books, 2020.

West, Kate. *The Real Witches' Year*. Element, 2004.

"The Freecycle Network." *Freecycle*, http://Freecycle.org.

"Where Spirituality, Politics, and Pop Culture Collide!" *The Magical Buffet*. http://themagicalbuffet.com.

Wildman, Laura. *Celebrating the Pagan Soul*. Citadel Press, 2005.

Wilson, Roberta. *Aromatherapy*. Avery, 2002.

"Witch School International." *Witch School*, http://witch-school.com.

"Witchcraft Store & Supplies." *Sacred Mists Shoppe*, http://Sacredmists.com.

Wood, Gail. *Rituals of the Dark Moon*. Llewellyn Worldwide, 2004.

——. *The Wild God*. Spilled Candy Publication, 2006.

Worwood, Valerie Ann. *The Complete Book of Essential Oils and Aromatherapy*. New World Library, 2016.

"Your Source for Wiccan, Pagan, Occult, Ritual and Spiritual Supplies." *Azure Green*, http://AzureGreen.com.

INDEX

H

I

J

K

L

MORE BY CROSSED CROW BOOKS

Circle, Coven, & Grove by Deborah Blake
The Way of Four by Deborah Lipp
Magic of the Elements by Deborah Lipp
Sleep and Sorcery by Laurel Hostak-Jones
Merlin: Master of Magick by Gordon Strong
The Bones Fall in a Spiral by Mortellus
Your Star Sign by Per Henrik Gullfoss
The Complete Book of Spiritual Astrology by Per Henrik Gullfoss
The Eye of Odin by Per Henrick Gullfoss
Icelandic Plant Magic by Albert Bjorn
The Black Book of Johnathan Knotbristle by Chris Allaun
A Witch's Book of Terribles by Wycke Malliway
Death's Head by Blake Malliway
In the Shadow of Thirteen Moons by Kimberly Sherman-Cook
Witchcraft Unchained by Craig Spencer
Wiccan Mysteries by Raven Grimassi
Wiccan Magick by Raven Grimassi
A Victorian Grimoire by Patricia Telesco
Celtic Tree Mysteries by Steve Blamires
Star Magic by Sandra Kynes
Witches' Sabbats and Esbats by Sandra Kynes
A Spirit Work Primer by Naag Loki Shivanaath
A Witch's Shadow Magick Compendium by Raven Digitalis
Flight of the Firebird by Kenneth Johnson
Witchcraft and the Shamanic Journey by Kenneth Johnson
Travels Through Middle Earth by Alaric Albertsson
Be Careful What You Wish For by Laetitia Latham-Jones
The Wildwood Way by Cliff Seruntine
Ecstatic Witchcraft by Fio Gede Parma
Aisling by Jeremy Schewe
Mastering the Art of Witchcraft by Frater Barrabbas
Transformative Initiation for Witches by Frater Barrabbas
Sacramental Theurgy for Witches by Frater Barrabbas

Learn more at
www.CrossedCrowBooks.com